BACK YOURSELF

TRANSFORM CHALLENGE INTO CONFIDENCE

TOMMY GENTLEMAN

BALBOA.
PRESS
A DIVISION OF HAY HOUSE

Book and Cover design by Andy Evans with credit
to Mie the tattooer for the Dragon crest

Editing by Kirsten Rees ~ MakeMeASuccess

Print information available on the last page.

ISBN: 978-1-9822-8046-8 (sc)
ISBN: 978-1-9822-8045-1 (e)

Balboa Press rev. date: 01/10/2019

To my parents Jacqueline and Ivan, and to my wife Kelly. Thank you for having my back.

I would not be the Father or the "Gentleman" that I am today if it were not for the 3 of you.

CONTENTS

WELCOME

To the person who has been through challenge, struggle, or pain, I want you to know you are in the right place. This is the book that you read when you are ready to build your inner strength, happiness, and confidence.

Welcome to Back Yourself.

Throughout my career, there has been one stand out question I have been asked time and time again by clients, followers, and friends. "I want to learn how to feel, think, and be better...What book do you recommend to help me get started?"

I always struggled to find a book that would help connect the dots in a simple way whilst not pulling any punches in terms of its true meaning. There are plenty of amazing books out there, but I just didn't have an answer that straight up called out to the person who wanted to learn, grow, and do more; but had a limited exposure to the world of personal development.

I wrote this book with the intention of it becoming a bridge that can take someone from surface level motivation into the amazing world of personal development. I have been a student and teacher in the personal development space since 2008 and I can honestly say if it weren't for personal development, I would be unhappy, unhealthy, and miserable.

The personal development journey is an amazing one that brings so many insights, revelations, and breakthroughs. I'm excited for what you will learn and discover for yourself. I promise to give you my truth and always keep your best interests at heart. I won't sugar coat my message because I understand how confusing and frustrating it can be. Life can sting.

As humans, we are more stretched and stressed than ever before. The physical, mental, and emotional demands of the world we live in flow too fast for the capacity of our bucket. That is why we often need to go on holiday and rest from the stress of everyday life to avoid crashing and burning. It's why we reach for shiny, short-term, and shallow solutions to try and soothe our stress. Yet most of the time, these perceived solutions only add to the problem, compounding our negative experiences and self-doubt even deeper into a depression.

Diets, pills, alcohol, cigarettes, sex, addictive games, social media, and even crazy fitness plans are all evidence of us trying our absolute hardest to avoid going toe to toe with our challenges, instead reaching for temporary distraction, hormone release, and escapism. Every weekend, the vicious cycle eats away at our happiness. Our self-worth, self-esteem, and self-confidence take a hit every time and we end up wasting energy, opportunities, and time. The worst part is, we don't even know we are doing it. We think we are doing 'good' meanwhile, we are creating a deeper and more volatile problem.

So what has to happen for us to transform challenge into confidence? The good news is that you are the one who can do something about it. It doesn't matter how you feel right now because your past does not dictate your future. This is some of what I will help you with in this book. I will share long-term strategies you can integrate into your life to steer yourself towards happiness and good health. I will also share with you tips to create instant positive impact physically, mentally and emotionally right now, TODAY.

I **promise** you can live a healthy, happy, confident, and successful life, no matter what you've been through. I am not saying it will be easy, but it is possible that you can lift yourself up from any rut, challenge, or depression in your life and turn things around completely in order to live with energy, confidence, and abundance.

Happy, healthy, and high-performing people were not born that way. They learnt how to operate at a level which brings success no matter what happens and you can too. All of our ups and downs are relative and will challenge our spectrum of emotions in a way that is unique to us all. In other words, if they can do it, so can you.

My goal is to bring you closer with this book. Closer to confidence, closer to success, and closer to your 'Super Self.' I am going to share my experience and expertise with you to help you understand what has worked for me. I will combine my own personal stories with proven strategies and tips that I teach my clients week in week out.

I'm excited that we have connected at this time in your life. Things often work in a special way and my belief is that this is meant to be. Let me take this opportunity to invite you to reach out to me at any time throughout this book. The best ways, right now (in 2018 as I write this!) are:

Through Instagram or Twitter - @TommyGentleman
Via Email - tommy@backyourselfbook.com

It's also helpful during the process to regularly check in, document, and be accountable to your journey. Use the Hashtag **#BackYourselfShare** on social media to share your own thoughts or experiences as you progress through the book and beyond!

I will be keeping a close eye on your progress through this hashtag on social media and you might just connect with like-minded people along the way too!

Congratulations on making a really positive move. By holding this book, you've already started to **back yourself.**

START THE CHANGE

Einstein famously said, "the definition of insanity is doing the same thing and expecting a different result."

Confidence can grow as soon as you begin to break down your challenges. It's time to start disrupting the norm and doing things differently to find answers. The answers exist on the inside. They all demand time, energy, and focus in order to find them. Yet so many people are looking for the answers on the outside in the form of social acceptance and short-term satisfaction.

The issue is not the desire. It's where that desire is pointed. Deep down, you have that desire. You want happiness. It's inside of you. You feel it for yourself. That's why you're reading this book. The opportunity is just too big to ignore.

It's an absolute miracle that you are here. Sometimes, we can take the fundamental basics for granted. The earth is 4.5 billion years old and you are here now. Today. In an age where we are all connected. Where business ideas can be conceived and start making money within the same twenty-four hours. Your phone that has more potential for learning than any historical scholar, scientist, mathematician, philosopher or leader ever had at their disposal *(Imagine if Einstein had Google.)*

We all have the opportunity to be a part of something meaningful. To leave a legacy behind us, crafted by our everyday actions and connections with our fellow human beings. This is an amazing time to be alive. You had no choice over the situation and time to which you were born, but you do absolutely have a choice in how it pans out.

You are the creator.
You are the driver.
You are the artist.

PART ONE

The Back Yourself Journey

Everyone experiences a different flow of events in life. No life is the same as the next. Some people can go for years before they are happy, some people can go for years until they feel pain. It's unpredictable. However, what I can say for certain is that we all share the same spectrum of emotions and we are all presented with pivotal moments in our lives that shape and mould who we are.

To be able to 'Back Yourself' is to able to keep going, no matter what happens. To be able to enjoy the highest of highs and to fight for what you believe in through the lowest of lows. My own journey enabled me to learn how to back myself at a fairly early age, and for this I am grateful. For me, it all happened between ages eighteen and twenty.

These two years have become the foundations for my personal and professional life. What happened in my life in that time gave me a deeper thirst for learning and an extreme sensitivity to the clock. Time is ticking and I have been practising, studying, and executing the most effective self-development strategies ever since.

The need to 'Back Yourself' will always exist. It's a vital ingredient for success and victory in the battles we face throughout life. Today's enemy will not be the same as the enemy you face this time next year, or in ten years' time, but the need to back yourself will be a constant throughout the process.

In this chapter of the book, I will walk you through the journey that taught me the true meaning of the phrase 'back yourself'.

STEP OUT OF YOUR COMFORT ZONE

It's never pleasant and it's never easy. It can make us sweat, swear and often scares the pants off us, but every time you step out, you open up the possibility for self-development and growth.

There are no rules as to how it will happen. Each person's life is in equal proportion to the next. It doesn't have to be grand, it can be modest and simple. There is no league table and no comparison. Whether it's quitting a job you hate, moving out, asking that girl/guy out on a date, volunteering for something good, or simply choosing to wear a new colour; everyone's experience of stepping out of the comfort zone is equally meaningful.

Can you remember the first time you stepped outside of your comfort zone? Your ability to back yourself was born in *that moment.* For me, it was leaving my hometown as a 19-year-old, to go on a working holiday adventure in New Zealand.

I've been in the health and fitness industry since 2006. It's pretty much all I've ever known other than having a paper round, washing dishes, and doing some gardening as a teenager.

My career started in my local leisure centre as a gym instructor and after eight months of full-time employment, I took my mum up on her offer of going to New Zealand to visit my aunt and cousin. As well as the prospect of being in an incredible country, there was the added bonus that my aunt owned a gym. I saw it as a fantastic opportunity to gain some experience and learn more about running a business in the health and fitness industry.

I absolutely loved it and within days, I knew I wanted to stay for longer than three months. Although, the town was just a bit too small and comfortable. Too much like home. I knew if I was to make a go of it in New Zealand, I would have to move from small-town Rotorua to one of the bigger cities, to Auckland.

Once I was sure of my decision, I told my mum I wanted to stay and she started to cry. She said, "You're not gonna come back, are you?" If there was going to be a no turning back moment, this was it. I had to look into the teary eyes of my own mother and tell her, "Mum, there's too much opportunity out here for me. It would be a massive mistake to come home."

We both cried and hugged it out. She understood, and to this day she still backs everything I do and for that, I'm massively grateful. I knew when she sat on that plane home to my dad and my brother, she would be more proud of me than anything else.

I managed to get myself a job as a personal trainer at Les Mills New Lynn in West Auckland and secured myself some temporary accommodation near the gym. I had spent all of my money before I committed to staying and all I had in my possession was a backpack, sleeping bag, laptop, and a pillow I was kindly given by a new friend. I was starting a new life. A life detached from my parents and my brother. A life that was 100% my responsibility.

We should always look to say YES to exciting opportunities that come our way and sometimes you have to figure out the 'how' as you go. Exciting decisions in life will always require an element of risk. I had no idea what life would be like on my own on the other side of the world. I had a very limited range of life skills. I couldn't cook, had never been longer than seven days away from home, and I only knew a handful of people in the entire country.

On that first night in Auckland, sharing a house with strangers, the eighteen-year-old version of me lay on the cold floor of an empty room, and a sudden feeling of self-belief came over me. **This is what it feels like to 'step outside my comfort zone'.**

This was the start of a powerful two-year journey of personal development. Much like you at day one of your greatest challenge, I was completely naive to what the world had in store for me. The highs and the lows and everything else in between.

When you step outside of your comfort zone, you learn so much about yourself. When was the last time you were brave and stepped outside of yours? Maybe you already have or maybe you think you should? Whatever the answer, I invite you to approach life with the philosophy that if things are to change, they first require the courage to venture out into the unknown.

The next twenty-four months of my life would go on to teach me some powerful lessons that will help me to explain what it takes for you to 'back yourself'.

TAKE FULL RESPONSIBILITY

As we go through life we can get used to a certain level of comfort and entitlement. Entitlement is the enemy of responsibility. When we feel like we are entitled to something, it removes our need to take responsibility and shifts the control to someone or something else. Entitlement is an illusion. We are responsible for everything and at some point on our journey, we must learn this.

There are a number of things you will take for granted in your life. Things that you might think you are entitled to. It could be as simple as wifi at your local cafe or room service in a hotel. Or, it could be something more substantial like a roof over your head, running water, heating, or in my case a bed.

The first few weeks of my new job as a Personal Trainer were tough. I was learning so much and had very little money or belongings. It was such a contrast to what my life had been like in England. I was literally learning how to live as an adult. How to plan ahead, pay rent, do washing, cook food, and just generally organise myself. I didn't even know how to cook rice! I lived off of tinned tuna and protein shakes for the first few weeks.

I knew that I had to find some more suitable living conditions and soon enough a place became available and a colleague from the gym and I moved into a rented house together. It was a relief to be in a place I could call home, but I was still sleeping on the floor. That pillow my friend had given me was not only for sleeping on. It was also my sofa, my office chair, and my garden seat. The reality of life had kicked in and after rent, food, and fuel, money was tight.

I am sure you will agree, having a bed is a pretty fundamental possession in our modern-day culture. It is something we can very easily take for granted, but fundamentally, for me in my life I am grateful that having a bed is considered a standard living condition. I could only sleep on the floor for so long. Things needed to change and I had to start introducing some stability into my living conditions. Until I found more paying clients, I would struggle to buy any furniture.

One weekend, my housemate came home and told me one of his friends was moving to Dubai and had a house load of furniture to sell for cheap. Including a queen-sized bed for $250. At the time, that equated to around £100. An absolute bargain for a bed that would normally cost hundreds of dollars. Problem solved!

Well, there was one small issue. I had NO money and he needed to sell it fast. I knew the offer was too good to miss and so I did what I had always done when in a time of need. I called home and I asked for money.

Now, my parents brought me up to have a great understanding of money and the value of things. I was by no means spoilt, nor did I have a privileged upbringing, but what I did always have is unconditional love and support. Sometimes, based on the situation, that meant that my parents would lend me money if they deemed it fair and fit. I saw this situation as a real no-brainer. Precious, first-born son on the other side of the world needs to borrow £100 to buy a bed. A fundamental piece of furniture at an absolute bargain price.

My Mum picked up the phone. I told her about my situation and then I dropped the line, "So, can I please borrow £100 to pay for this bed as I haven't got any money at the moment". The phone went quiet for an awkward five seconds until my mum spoke, "I have just spoken to your father and the answer is no."

"No? Come on Mum, don't be silly, when can you send me the money?" I could have sworn that she was joking.

Then I heard my dad's voice, "Tom, listen, you either figure out how to earn some more money or you fly home. It's as simple as that. We have given you too much money and now you have to figure it out for yourself."

His words down the phone gave me a serious dose of reality. I had become too big for my boots and let pride get in the way of progress. The truth is, the gym had offered me some paid work as an instructor while I set up my PT business. I said no because I thought I didn't need it. I thought that I was too good to take a step backwards and work as a gym instructor. I thought that I was ENTITLED to earn more money as a PT. I was done with wiping down machines and working long hours for a quarter of the price as a 'just a' gym instructor. My pride had got ahead of my true self, but from his kitchen in the UK, my Dad straightened me out.

He was serious about his message. He wanted an update the next day. He told me to get money in as soon as possible and act immediately on his words if I wanted the bed, and ultimately, if I wanted to stay in NZ. It was very clear I would not be receiving any more money from my parents to help fund my way in NZ.

When I look back now, I appreciate this lesson so much. It was brave of my mum and dad to take this approach and I am grateful they taught me a lesson that may have exposed a dependency and weakness if I didn't learn it when I did. I would have remained in the mindset of entitlement. Expecting to be bailed out and shifting the responsibility onto other people.

Needless to say, the next day I went to the gym and signed up for some hours as a gym instructor. The hourly rate was fifty percent less than as a Personal Trainer. A gym shift would be eight hours long and often a five am start or an eleven pm finish. It was a necessary move and I had to swallow my pride. After a week, I had enough money to buy the bed.

You must learn to take full responsibility for every shortcoming in life.

Nothing is guaranteed.

It's up to YOU.

Nobody else.

QUIT COMPLAINING

The journey between successful events and testing times can often contain valuable hidden lessons. When things are 'normal', we can get a bit frustrated at the lack of action. It is within these stages that we must learn to create our own progress and stop complaining. When we learn to stop complaining, we can become even more self-aware and self-awareness is an essential ingredient for continued success.

In 2009, personal training was starting to boom. It had broken into the industry as something for everybody, rather than just for celebrities and wealthy people. More and more people were seeing the job as a way to earn a decent living doing something they love. I saw this opportunity as soon as I entered the fitness industry and now I was finally living it, charging great money for work that didn't even feel like a job. People were always interested when I told them what I did for a living as it was a job role that many people saw as illustrious and highly rewarding. Two weeks later and I felt the complete opposite!

I had only one client who had paid for ten sessions upfront. I'd already burned through the money and as a result, had to take on shifts as a Gym Instructor to make ends meet. It was on one of these shifts that I learned that SUCCESS is no coincidence.

One of the Personal Trainers at the gym at the time had a reputation for being the best PT, with the most clients and the most MONEY. He drove a flash sports car, had the latest smartphone, and would often be seen counting his cash. Initially, I thought he was ignorant and cocky. I hadn't had much opportunity to talk to him in the couple of weeks I had been there. Probably because he was too busy getting paid.

Then one day, on one of my quiet gym shifts, he was sat in the main gym on his phone. I went and sat down next to him. He said nothing.

I sighed and said, "There's literally nothing to do, I'm so bored."

He said nothing. So, in an attempt to beat the awkward silence, I said: "Jesus, doing gym shifts is so shit and boring."

To which he interrupted me without even lifting his eye gaze from his phone and said, "Well maybe, if you went and actually spoke to people instead of sitting here, wasting my time with your complaints, you might actually have some clients and you wouldn't have to do gym shifts anymore."

Initially, I wanted to punch him in the face! But after a few seconds, his message sank in, and I decided he was right. I was complaining and wasting time, when instead, I could be doing something to directly affect and change the exact situation I was complaining about.

For the next three days, I spoke to as many gym users as possible, finding out what they were training for and how I could help them succeed. I picked up six new clients and told my boss I no longer needed to do the gym shifts. Those six clients stayed with me the whole time I was out in New Zealand and formed the backbone of my business, allowing me to pay rent, buy food, and put fuel in my car.

Becoming more self-aware can be a powerful thing, when you can be honest with yourself and take action instead of complaining you will begin to see changes. You will evolve your attitude to steer all aspects of your life towards success.

You are the one in control of your attitude.

EXPRESS YOUR UNIQUE IDENTITY

As time passes we continue to build and understand who we are on a conscious and unconscious level. We form an IDENTITY and behave in alignment with what we believe in. We start to express ourselves more as we ground our understanding of how we show up in the world and continue to figure out our own unique meaning towards life. We can do this through the clothes we wear, the places we eat, the way we style our hair, the types of music we listen to, and even with body art.

It's these choices in life that allow us to extend the reach of our uniqueness into the awareness of others and project the evidence that we are all different. Being on my own in a new country, on the other side of the world, and single for the first time as an adult gave me limitless possibilities to get out there and do things. I was literally accountable to no one.

My self-expression was taking shape. My support network had grown, I had a handful of great friends, knew my way around, and even joined a local football team. The thrill of building a new 'adult' identity had empowered me. Self-expression creates a stronger connection of self-confidence. For me, it was a Maori tattoo.

A few of the other trainers at the gym had got themselves one to mark their journey and express their own unique message. The thought of a Maori tattoo on my body seemed like a really powerful and magical thing.

Things were great and I had built a life for myself. I was falling in love with New Zealand. The Maori culture had gripped me and I was fortunate enough to have been invited to a ceremonious Maori dinner or "hongi" as it's known as. This is a traditional method of cooking where the meat is cooked underground by the heat of the earth and then pulled up after a few hours.

I had been in NZ for nine months and felt like I had figured out my identity. I had learnt who I was and caught up for the time that I had been sheltered from inner growth by living at home comfortably and being in a relationship that was more suppressing than expressing at the latter stages. I was single, independent, and free. My confidence was high and I was ready to express my love for life, family and adventure. The process was enlightening.

Tattoo is deep in Maori culture and they take it very seriously. For years, they have used tattoo as a ceremonious way of communicating. A language amongst tribes to tell a story of their purpose, history, and honour to the land. Sometimes, when a young man is given permission to be tattooed by an Elder, it symbolizes his coming of age and acceptance within the tribe from boy to man.

My chest tattoo took a total of nine hours over two days. On the first day, I walked in and was greeted by the artist with open arms. He said, "So, are you ready to become a man?"

He wanted to make sure that I was deserving of his art and energy. He spent an hour with me talking again about what I wanted to express in my tattoo. He told me more about Maori tattoo culture and explained how the traditional method of Maori tattoo is called "Ta Moko" and uses a chisel approach to 'tap' into the skin and leave a permanent inking. Traditionally, this chisel would have been carved from Albatross bone and the Ta Moko ceremony would have included many rites and rituals. It would have been a big deal for all involved, especially the family. Men would traditionally have Ta Moko on their faces, thighs, and buttocks, whereas women would have their lips and chins marked. A true Maori tattoo is always a unique piece of art.

Due to being English and not a resident or indeed Maori myself, he advised me that he could never use the Ta Moko chisel method and would instead use the modern tattoo gun approach. He also told me he would include wave designs to symbolise that I was a traveller embracing their special culture.

I loved how authentic he was and how he was 'playing by the rules' of his heritage and history. He made sure that he took this approach with tourists because he has a deep love and respect for his culture. So much so that he will protect its sacred traditions.

He drew the art onto my chest with a pen and made me sit in front of a mirror for thirty minutes. He told me, "You have thirty minutes to get used to seeing something that you will see forever."

As I sat there, looking at myself in the mirror, I had a chance to reflect on my journey and life in general. I had followed my instincts to be where I was leaving a job, a relationship, and my family to come on an adventure. I had set myself up financially, doing a job that I loved, and I had met some incredible people.

I wanted my tattoo to represent bravery and adventure. I also wanted to include my parents and my brother in the tattoo, as wherever I go in the world and in life, I can take them with me. This was important to me as it was the ONLY thing that ever distracted my desire to be in NZ. I wanted my family with me on the journey.

I was about to embark on a process that would mark this message on my body for life. Surrounded by the tradition and culture of this amazing country, the arena for my growth in becoming a man. The time had come and I was ready to be inked. The artist said a Maori prayer out loud and then played a song loudly through the studio speakers. The song contained some strong and powerful Maori chants, fused with drum beats and tribal sounds.

I closed my eyes and invited the power into my body. I felt the needle on my skin and it ignited a purpose within me. I can only explain it as an incredible blend of meaning. For the first time, I felt like my life was in my hands. I realized that I had complete control of my situation and that I was the navigator of my own fate. It's something you have to feel as a result of the invisible cord being cut from your nurtured upbringing.

Self-expression happens in different ways for different people. Some faster than others, but all of us need this release at some point in our early adult years. The last year had been such a thrilling adventure. I now had something permanent on my body to remind me of it forever. I felt it. I was my own man.

Your self-expression is so important. It's an intimate internal dialogue that you can share with the rest of the world. You get to choose how you show up and how to share your beliefs and values with the world. You get to be creative and illustrate your identity.

As this identity takes its maturity, you start to really know 'who you are' and your confidence grows. It is an important stage in reaching your full potential as this new confidence will open up opportunities for you that previously would have been ignored.

I am not saying you need to get a tattoo. It can be something very simple.

How can you express yourself fully today?

BE READY TO PIVOT

I had no choice. It would be illegal for me to stay and work any longer on my current visa. A year had passed already and my application to stay for a further 3 years had been declined. The reason being, that as a self-employed Personal Trainer, my income wasn't technically safe or guaranteed. New Zealand immigration department prefer you to have an employed position and an employer who can sponsor you a job. I was disappointed and frustrated but then I soon learned to accept what I couldn't control and began to think about what the future looked like for me.

Whenever we are presented with a situation that conflicts with our 'ideal' desired outcome, we must break all of the elements apart and look at every single aspect of the problem objectively. There was nothing I could do about my visa situation. "It is what it is," I told myself.

Letting go of what you cannot control is difficult but it's the only way you can proceed positively. The removal of the disappointment and frustration allows us to see things clearly and streamline our thinking. The best thing we can do is to create a new meaning for the situation, a meaning that focuses on opportunity.

The biggest opportunity in coming home was seeing my little brother grow up and to be with him through his teens. This became my new narrative for coming home. "I am coming home for my brother. For Jamie."

The last few months in Auckland felt lonely. It was almost like my life was a temporary existence, caught in the middle between a learning experience and a solid future. I felt I was being pulled back home. It's amazing what happens to your motivation when you alter the meaning of your movements.

Now I knew I was coming home, I had one eye on my exit strategy. I worked hard and earned as much money as possible during the last few months. I wanted to travel the South Island before I left NZ. I needed to raise around $4,000 to pay for my travel, accommodation, flights home, and to settle the phone contract and the house rental agreement that I had signed myself into thinking that I would be staying for the long-term!

Whenever we are presented with a need to earn money, we must do whatever it takes to maximise our opportunities and cash flow. There are so many ways we can earn money. Money is an energy flow. We are rewarded for the effort, service, and time we give to something, by a currency; money. There are always more options available to us than just our regular wages.

In my case, I sold my client base to a fellow PT, sold some of my belongings, and decided to move back to Rotorua with my aunt. Not only would I have no rent to pay, my aunt Jeni had the gym and there were opportunities to make a quick buck over a month doing some boot camps and teaching group fitness classes.

I also managed to earn some extra money working in a bar. This was something I had always wanted to do and allowed me to live a different lifestyle for a while. One of regular drinking, late nights, and comradery. I suppose having to live such a mature life so quickly into my adulthood had left a craving for more of a care-free lifestyle. I wanted to get this out of my system before coming home.

I managed to save up enough money to go on a bus tour around the country. New Zealand is a relatively small country with a population of around 4.6 million people and 1.5 million of those people live in Auckland. The travel experience, itself, was like no other. I was a free spirit on this bus. A new town every day. New environments, new people, new stories, and new experiences. It really is a great way to learn about the world from the inside out. I lived it up. Boy, did I have fun. Too much fun to write in this book!

I had decided to keep my homecoming a secret. As far as my family back home were concerned, I was moving back to Jeni's house for a few months to work at her gym. The grand plan was to return home and surprise my family at my mum's 50th birthday party.

The airport is like a magic portal of discovery and adventure. The small area of carpet outside the departures lounge may as well be called the floor of tears. A passage in and out of this small but beautiful country that so many people form a loving connection to.

In the eighteen months I had spent in New Zealand I had said goodbye to my mum, my ex-girlfriend, two friends, and even my cousin on the very same patch of carpet. Now it was my turn to hand in my ticket and walk through the departures archway to board a plane out of the country. I said goodbye to my NZ family a few days before my departure day. They were never big fans of goodbyes and it worked out better logistically for me to go alone.

I stood on that 'carpet of tears' and looking back at the departure lounge. People were embracing and saying their goodbyes. Some excited and smiling, some upset and sad. I thought about all of the people who I had met since arriving. All of the small and seemingly insignificant days of what was known to be normal life added up to form a proud pattern of achievement.

I felt a cocktail of strong emotions, as I stood caught in the vacuum between my past and my future. "How could a country have such an impact?"

I realised the answer to this question was a metaphor for life. Time ticks by each and every day and if you say YES to opportunities and follow your heart, you are rewarded with an incredible spectrum of human emotion and experience.

I took a deep breath, knowing it would not be the last time I journeyed to this place where I had come of age. It's easy to dwell on the disappointment but sometimes things don't work out the way we initially wanted them to. I had every intention to stay in New Zealand for another three years and eventually apply for residency but it wasn't to be. When things don't go your way, you must immediately begin looking for other opportunities. There will always be more than you first think.

It all depends on the lens that you look through. One way to tackle these situations is to use the lens of fun. Ask yourself, "What is the most exciting possibility amongst my options?" For me, it was coming home and surprising my whole family in the middle of my Mum's 50th birthday party.

SHOW GRATITUDE & LOVE

There I was outside the party venue waiting for my cue from the DJ. I had sent him an audio clip to play over the speakers, explaining how sorry I was that I couldn't be there. I heard my voice play over the speakers. There were goosebumps all over my body. Partly from the excitement, partly from the cold. This was it. I was going to see my family. The three people I loved the most.

I walked in, and it was one of the best moments of my life. My Dad greeted me first and gave me a huge hug. I looked over to see my Mum walking towards me with her hands over her mouth. She was so shocked to see me. She slapped me on the chest and said, "What are you doing here?" Then she cried as she grabbed me and held me tightly in a way only a mother can. I closed my eyes and squeezed. When I opened my eyes, I saw my brother Jamie.

He was crying, struggling to wipe the tears. His face was a joy to see. He had grown a little taller and his hair was styled in a trendy fashion. He was hesitant to come to me, almost as if he was patiently waiting his turn, overwhelmed by unexpected emotion. The release of hurt and loneliness coupled with the joy of being reunited. I will always remember the look on his face. He was so happy to see his big brother, he was so proud of me.

It was one of the best moments of my life, and when I look back at the video footage, I can't help but feel a very heightened and raw sense of emotion. The four of us were together again. Smiling, crying and embracing.

I was glad that I had put in the effort to make it a special time for me, and my mum, my dad, and my brother. Our best moments in life stack up to form our fondest memories. I'm so grateful we shared that moment in time together. Our souls and our bodies together in such an embrace of love and union. None of us knew at the time, that this would be one of the last times we would be together as a four.

When things are good, it is important to step back, take a look, and be grateful. As far as we know, the best days of our lives could be the days that we are living RIGHT NOW. This philosophy is always applicable, on the basis that every moment in time is equal and although things could be better, they could also be worse.

Although it isn't productive to count on something bad happening at any time, we never really know what is around the corner. Terrible things can happen to anyone at any time. We cannot protect ourselves or anyone else from this potentially devastating scale of unpredictability.

I can't protect you but what I can do is emphasise the importance of gratitude and living in the now so that if and when you do hit some turbulence, you have enough strength, hope, and love around you to pull through. Living in the moment with gratitude and love made it possible for me to back myself and pull through it. The next part of my story includes hands down the hardest and most devastating time of my life.

It felt great to be home. The young, carefree teenager had grown up to be a young carefree man. I'd had the experience of living and surviving on my own in New Zealand and now I was back in little Andover. Back with a bag full of business ideas and fresh energy. The entrepreneur inside of me had been born. I was ready to create a fitness empire and I was really looking forward to making a go of things.

I lived life with a smile, making the most of it all. I remember playing in the snow, having snowball fights, and spending quality time with my brother Jamie. I was grateful to be back and able to watch him grow into a young adult. He was almost fourteen years old and had started to develop his own unique personality. Growing up, it had often been difficult to relate to one another fully, as we have almost seven years difference between us.

The way he would look at me with his innocent and almost worshipful eyes is one of the greatest blessings that an older brother can have. Yet at the time, it would have been an inconvenience! Even though I would often see him as 'the annoying little Brother' when I was trying to be cool with my friends, I always gave Jamie 100% of my love and time when it was just the two of us.

We grew up such happy kids. Jamie was this little bundle of energy that I'd watched mature, and grow, and learn, and I was so proud of him. Hanging out with him after a year and a half away was just awesome. He had a new-found independence that wasn't there before I left for New Zealand. He was growing up, and I wanted to be there to help him do it with a smile. This small phase of my life was probably one of the best. I was high on life. Buzzing with energy, confidence and ambition. My life was perfect.

It lasted for 44 days.

SURVIVE THROUGH THE DARKEST DAYS

On Saturday, March 15th, 2009, my younger brother Jamie suddenly passed away from a heart condition that nobody knew he had. This was just five days before his fourteenth birthday.

This was, without a doubt, the worst day of my life. My little brother. So much energy and so much potential, taken away from us in an instant. I was broken. My family was broken. The community were broken. I had gone from ecstatically happy to the lowest of lows overnight. At the time, I couldn't even fathom a day in the future where I would smile, let alone admit to being happy again.

The last day that we had together, I can remember waking up on the Saturday, and I could hear him and my dad arguing because my dad was still in bed. They were just playing. They always used to do this. Jamie had a football match, and he was worried he was going to be late. I remember opening my eyes, and the sunlight coming through the bedroom window, and thinking to myself, "I should probably go and watch this game. I could stay in bed, but I think I'm gonna get up and go watch this game."

Dad and Jamie left the house to go to the game. Once I heard them leave, I got up and got ready, and I drove there just in time for kickoff. I watched the game, seeing my young brother, almost fourteen years old, showing so much maturity. I'd said to him before the game, "Look, you're the captain of the team. Today, when you speak to your team, think about saying constructive instructions. Not just shouting, 'Come on, lads'." He really took it on board, because I could hear him talking about where people should stand, what they should do when they got the ball, strategic plays they should focus on. He had always been the best in his team and he was so passionate. He left many parents on the sidelines lost for words with his free kick specials and corner kicks that used to fly over everyone's heads and off for a throw in the other side. He hated losing but would always shake hands after the game. Just like a Gentleman should.

The game was locked at 0:0 with around ten minutes to go and something magical happened. The ball went up into the air on the edge of their box. I heard him shout, "Jamie's ball!" He chested the ball down, let it bounce once, and he thumped it. The ball screamed into the top corner of the net. He looked straight over at me and my dad and he celebrated with his arms out, his teammates clinging onto him and mobbing him in celebration. I can still remember jumping onto the pitch. It was that good. It was a true captain's performance. His team, Clatford Under 14s won that game, one nil with J. Gentleman the goal scorer. What a great decision it was to get up and watch the game.

I left before the team and went off to the gym. Later that day when we were both at home, I saw my opportunity to go and speak to Jamie about the game. At the time, he was playing on the Xbox. The TV was up high on a cabinet so he used to sit on the dining room table to get a better viewing angle when he played. He was sat on the table, looking at the screen when I walked in.

He had grown so much. He was just a young man growing up, figuring out his life just like I was. Like most teenagers, he had his concerns and challenges; and he had things in his life that gave him happiness. Football was one of these things, and so was playing the Xbox. Apparently, another was speaking to his big bro, because when I started talking to him about the match, he quit the game, took off his headset and put his controller down.

We spoke about the match. I told him how well he had done to step up and be a great leader. He had done all of the things I recommended him to do before the game, he had listened, applied and excelled. Scoring the winning goal in a 1:0 win means that you were the difference required to WIN the game. I told him how impressed I was and then I ended the conversation.

I turned and left the room. As I walked out through the door of the dining room, I cannot explain what it was, but…SOMETHING told me to stop. Like an invisible wall in front of me stopping me from walking forwards and urging me from my core to turn around and go tell Jamie what I really wanted to say.

He had already started to play his game again. The headset was on, controller in hand, and concentration face was in motion. My inner gut feeling was telling me to go back into that room, and say the words, "I'm proud of you." I questioned it in my head, and thought, 'Don't be so stupid. That's so mushy. There's no need for that. I've told him that he did well today, that's all that is necessary.'

But the other voice, the more powerful one with a very serious tone said, 'No. You need to tell him that you're proud of him.' I don't know why, but I listened to that voice that day and I will be forever grateful that I did. I managed to create a moment of love and true expression. Little did I know, it would be my last ever chance to do so.

I walked back into the room, smiled, ruffled his hair a little bit, and said, "I'm proud of you today." He took his eyes away from the screen, looked me in the eyes, and he smiled back at me. I know at that point in his life, in his own little world right there, that would've been the best thing that he could ever hear from his big brother.

Around eleven pm that night, I was in the line to get into the local nightclub, and my phone rang. It was my mum. I thought the usual thing, 'What does my mum want at this time of night.'

I picked up the phone. She didn't sound right, and my immediate thought was something had happened. She said to me, "You need to come now. Your brother's not well. I'm in an ambulance with him." And at that point, I just ran. I ran home as fast as I could.

At no point did we ever think that the impossible was possible. Here we were, in the emergency department of Winchester Hospital, standing in the 'Family Room' waiting to hear what the hell was going on.

After a long ten minutes, the door opened and in walked a doctor. He didn't look right either. He said, "There's no easy way to say this…"

The rest is too painful for me to describe, but I think you understand. For me, in my life, at that moment, all I wanted to do was wake up. It must be a dream. I was angry, I was punching the walls, I was crying and screaming, and I just wanted to wake up.

YOUR POTENTIAL, POWER, & PURPOSE

Nothing hits harder than the unexpected death of somebody you love. It stings and grinds everything to a sudden halt. The biggest test of strength is that even in these darkest of days we must apply the same philosophies of choice and attitude. Nothing can change what has happened once it has taken place. So therefore, all we really can do is cling on to anything at all that gives us even a glimpse of hope until the rawness of the event settles enough for us to be able to begin living life again, or at least start to figure out what the new normal looks like.

After the initial phase of mourning, it was time to start again. The love and support around me at that tough time gave me just about enough energy to be able to rebuild. I had a new appreciation for my own life.

As hard as it was, I had accepted the devastating event could never be changed, and the only thing that could, was the way in which I lived my life from there on in. A new philosophy was born and with it a new meaning.

I'm one of two children to my mum and dad, Ivan and Jacqui. I see it that I had a 50/50 chance. My brother passed away, and I'm still here. I know if it had been the other way around, and I could give him a message from beyond life, I would say to him, "You need to go and live your life now, for the both of us. You need to go and take all the opportunities that come your way. You need to build and become someone you can be proud of, and that other people can be proud of. You can help people and fully realise your potential." That's what I would say.

Everything stems from the core foundation, that I have an opportunity of life because I am still here, I can still do what I want to do, I can still make a difference, and I live my life for both of us.

I live my life to make him proud and because I can. It would be an insult to him, and anyone else who's no longer with us physically, if I was to waste the opportunity of my life, my time that I've been given to do what I want to do, and need to do with my time.

It's the same for you. I know there are people in your life that are no longer with us. You need to embrace that as an opportunity to go and live in their name and do the best that you possibly can to create a legacy. Think how powerful it would be if you were able to say to them in the afterlife or whatever you believe in, "Look, the reason I did those great things was because you inspired me. You inspired me to be more. By the way you lived your life, you inspired me to do great things, or to at least give it my best shot because that's how I view it."

CHANGE THE MEANING

When Jamie passed away it amplified my purpose and awakened something very powerful inside of me. Being such a popular boy and from a well-known family, there were floods of people in attendance to pay their respects to his life.

Speaking at a funeral is never ever an easy thing, especially when it's someone you love so much. The moment of light, hope, and power came as I stood in front of seven-hundred people.

I had a previous experience of this when I was fourteen years old, and my Nan passed away. As the oldest grandchild, I said I would speak at her funeral. I got up there, wearing a borrowed suit, and only managed two words before I choked and my dad had to save me. He had stood next to me while I cried into my hands. I thought that I'd made a fool of myself and let everybody down.

It stuck with me, and so when Jamie passed away, I just knew that I had to speak at his funeral. I had no notes. I just spoke from the heart. As I looked out at the faces staring back at me, I saw a full range of emotion and what I can only describe as beautiful waves of energy.

I felt confident and comfortable. It felt like I was doing the right thing, at the right moment in time. As I walked back to my seat in the front row of the church, I turned to look at the memorial photo of Jamie displayed at the altar.

"Now I have just done that, I can do anything. NOTHING else will ever be as hard or as testing as what I have just done. I fear nothing."

Within every negative event is the opportunity to become stronger, and in the deepest, darkest days of hurt, is the potential to discover your greatest power and purpose. I've translated the biggest and worst event in my life into the fuel for me to get everything I want to get done. It is the vehicle that brings me closer every single day towards fulfilling my full potential. You too can change the meaning of your struggle into the catalyst for your own greatness.

You can see beyond the clouds of hurt and pain to see the power, purpose, and potential. You are blessed with the opportunity of life. Your hardest challenges in life can one day become your greatest glory in the story of your life. It's a mindset that some never become exposed to. You have been exposed to the possibilities and now you can start to build and strengthen this mindset through conscious and unconscious conditioning.

Your unconscious mind is the archive of your emotions. You will store your memories in your unconscious mind, and it may even block out the most hurtful memories in an attempt to protect you. The unconscious mind is like an extremely fertile garden, and every time something happens, every time you feel something, a seed is planted. If a big, nasty, negative, seed is planted in your garden, it will grow into an ugly weed. You've got to be able to dig that weed out from the root, and re-soil. Get ready to plant something else in its place. Doing so requires a lot of courage.

Releasing our pain is tough, but when we show vulnerability, express ourselves fully, and create new perspectives and meanings towards past events, we are able to clear the weeds from the garden. We can create anything because we're always in control of our own attitude. We can plant gratitude for life. We can plant happiness. We can plant love.

It won't be easy, but it is possible and here are some simple ways to start the shift.

- Appreciate the little things, never take anything or anyone for granted
- Speak your words when they matter the most
- See the beauty in every single human being, each one of us is unique and equal
- Ask yourself WHAT you can do to help instead of WHY has this happened to me
- Say yes to getting out the house and doing things
- Write your thoughts and feelings down in a journal
- Surround yourself with people who lift you up
- Fall in love with life every day

Whatever life has dealt you so far, know that you are not alone and that you can choose to be happy. I am not here to tell you how to live your life. I hope sharing my story has brought you experience and perspective that you can relate to and inspiration to challenge your thinking.

I used my new found power and purpose and dedicated my life to helping other people find theirs. I've committed over a decade of my life towards learning and teaching health, happiness, and confidence.

This experience and expertise were captured through:

1. Studying the physical body
2. Studying mindset and NLP
3. Continuing my martial arts journey
4. Reading books on spirituality
5. Studying personal development from some of the best in the world

6. Travelling and experiencing new things with people
7. Running a business and growing it every year
8. Competing and pushing myself in multiple sports and discipline
9. Consistently taking breaks to reflect and evaluate
10. Staying in tune and self-aware throughout
11. Being a practitioner of health and high-performance
12. Setting my own standards high
13. Plus being a practitioner of life!

In the upcoming chapters, I will be sharing with you some proven and practical strategies that can help you to live a healthy, happy, and confident life. Methods that will help you to perform as your best, your "Super Self", no matter what happens.

Back Yourself Share #BackYourselfShare

What is the number one thing that you have taken from this book so far? Share your thoughts or perhaps a photo on social media and use our hashtag so I can connect with you!

PART TWO

Become Your Super Self

WHAT IS YOUR SUPER SELF?

Super Self is a philosophy.

I've built two events, a podcast, and a coaching academy on the foundations of this way of life. Your Super Self is you at your absolute best. That means you feel your best, look your best, and behave your best. Life is far too precious to be anything less than your best. If you had the choice or you could wave a magic wand and be whatever you wanted to be, would you not choose to be the best you can? So never settle for less and set the bar high. In fact, set the bar as high as you possibly can. You're incredible!

There will never be anyone else like you, EVER. Out of the billions of human beings that have existed since the dawn of time, none of them have been the same as you. There's only one YOU. You're a miracle.

Those who live as their Super Self are able to marry the acceptance of that miracle with a committed attitude to perform at the highest levels in life. To always show up and do your best.

The way I see it, one more person striving for the Super Self philosophy, is one more amazing individual grabbing the opportunity of life and backing themselves to live with energy, vibrancy, and passion. One more person showing up in the world as a better mother, father, sister, brother, cousin, uncle, aunt, colleague, friend, and lover. A powerful ripple effect occurs when somebody lives life as their Super Self.

You have to do this. The opportunity is just too big to miss. You can choose to become this version of you through what you do, your actions, your behaviours, and how you channel your thoughts, mindset, energy, and confidence. You can connect it to what you believe in and your deepest purpose in life. Bind this philosophy to what you're fighting for, and cement it inside of your strongest reason why you are alive.

Your life has the potential to be energetic, positive, and optimistic. You have the potential to bounce back from any challenge that life throws at you, including the one that you find yourself in right now. I truly believe this and I know it because I've been there myself, and I've helped many people to come out from a place of darkness and depression to then find happiness and good health.

What if you were able to steadily grow over the next few months in order to create a complete shift in reality? You will still be the same human being but in a completely different place. I want you to be able to enjoy looking in the mirror; knowing that whatever happens today, happens as the Super Self.

SUPER SELF TRAITS

- Showing up as the best possible version of you in every given situation.
- Knowing that you are a work-in-progress and that's ok.
- Accepting your weaknesses but going all-in on your strengths.
- Deploying unlimited love to yourself first, then sharing that love with other people without expectation.
- Always being a student first and then a teacher.
- Allowing imagination to flow and drive ideas every single day.
- To always see the opportunity in every moment.
- Accepting choice and responsibility for every inconvenience and victory.
- Treating your body with the respect it deserves; it's your unique and marvellous vehicle of movement and life.
- To communicate from the heart and never hold back.
- Striving to marry the head, the heart, and the hands.
- Understanding that there is energy in everything and you are responsible for the energy you bring.

YOUR HIGHEST LEVELS OF LIFE PERFORMANCE

High life performance is all about achieving your absolute best use of time, energy and focus. To become a master of all three is to become a master of productivity, power, and progress.

Ever wonder how some people can get so much done in so little time? Or how they can give so much energy to people yet still have enough to maintain high standards and quality in their own life? It's through the self-development of high-performance.

Our time, energy, and focus are tested and stretched by external factors around us. Our jobs, family commitments, situational demands, social pressures, distractions, confusion, lack of belief, and our past experiences to name a few. The goal is to maintain an even keel with regards to the 'run of the mill' necessary demands of life, whilst separating enough time, energy, and focus to concentrate on the projects and actions that are required in order to keep moving forwards and achieving results. All whilst making sure the narrative is a positive one and that everything is conducted in the essence of happiness.

It's not simple. It is essentially the game of life and to win, you must be willing to work, learn and make sacrifices. High-performance is about recognizing what is important, delegating, sharing, communicating, and executing. It is about overcoming procrastination and ensuring all of your actions add up to create your desired success and happiness. High-performance is essentially what I teach people on a daily basis and in this book, I will be sharing many of the fundamental lessons I teach my clients.

We are talking about skills that are learnt over time through repetition, reinforcement, and conditioning. There is a reason that the world's top performers are at the top and the best at what they do. They chose to be the best they possibly can be and with that desire, they committed to mastering their own high-performance every single day, through all the ups and downs.

You are in the process of mastering yours. It's a journey that requires commitment and a dedicated approach towards learning. It demands courage and the willingness to go above and beyond. There may be competition along the way, but the biggest competition always lies within yourself. It's about being that little bit better than yesterday. That way, it's inevitable that you'll move forwards and continue to perform at your highest level.

PATIENCE IS KEY

If every diet or workout plan came with a warning, 'MAY TAKE MONTHS BEFORE YOU SEE A REAL RESULT', what do you think would happen? Nobody would do it! If it were easy, everyone would be rich and ripped.

For decades, we have had a cultural desire to have results as fast as possible. I mean, why would you want to spend another day in discomfort when a solution is right there, in a box, a pill, or a program? The unfortunate side effect of people WANTING to feel good about their body and mind, is that a huge supply vs. demand cyclone of opportunity exists for people to market a solution to the desperation in the market.

You cannot rush a masterpiece and your body is the ultimate masterpiece. It is a unique and incredible organism whose potential far exceeds its significance in size. It has taken thousands of years of evolution to get things to right NOW.

So today, I urge you to evolve your thinking and change any narrative inside of you that is looking for a short-term solution or a quick fix. Your body and therefore your health is yours until the day you die. You don't cast your body away when you're bored of it or fancy doing something else. It isn't like a hobby or a part-time phase. Your body really is LIFE itself.

You're in this for life so it's time to start thinking about things on a macro, long-term level. The key is to make a bigger picture plan and then back that plan up with at least one micro-action every single day. Apply patience to this self-development process.

Patience is a key ingredient to any success in life that is truly worth having. Patience is the shadow of success.

THE GIFT OF CHOICE

We are all born equally neutral in our emotional set. Other than some minor perceptions of the 'outside world' picked up in the womb, we are born ready to learn what human experience is all about. We rely on others to teach us. Our parents, guardians, siblings, school teachers, coaches, friends, and family members. The influence we receive from these people helps us to form our personality and to discover our own path in life.

There comes a point where we may have to look beyond the random situational opportunities that we were born into and look further afar for the answers. Once we flip this switch, we gain control of our learning experience. We can look to books, mentors, and the internet to discover new skills and learnings that will benefit our greater plan and goals in life. We can start to shape and mould who we are by what we know and more importantly, what we DO with that knowledge.

Knowledge alone isn't power. It's the application of that knowledge that holds all the power. Self-development is the ultimate way to learn. So, for the remainder of this book, I invite you to approach with an open mind and to embrace the imagination that exists inside of you. The imagination that you've had since you were young, but may be turned down or completely switched off in adulthood.

Even in the deepest of ruts, there exists opportunity for good. The spectrum of choice will vary and stretch from one situation to the next

but make no mistake, it ALWAYS exists. Human life is consciousness and consciousness is choice. This same choice is present in everything from the food that goes in your mouth to the way you approach your darkest days.

#BackYourselfShare

What are you going to do today to show up as your 'Super Self?' Remember, it doesn't have to be big but it does have to be positive. Share a post or a photo so the 'Back Yourself Community' and I can see your statement!

Back Yourself BONUS!

Head over to www.backyourselfbook.com/bonus for a bonus coaching video series to help you with your journey!

PART THREE

The Back Yourself
Beliefs

The following 'Back Yourself Beliefs' are methods, mindsets, and philosophies that will help you get through your day-to-day challenges. Whether it be a small obstacle or a life-altering event, these are the tools that will empower you to pull through. I have used these Back Yourself Beliefs at various points in my life and I've also used them to help thousands of other people.

Now you can use them to keep moving forwards, to keep progressing, to keep your head above water, and eventually reap an abundance of health, happiness, and success.

SET THE BAR HIGH

There are no rules as to how high you can aim. One thing that is for sure is that the level of your success will never be higher than the standards you set yourself. Therefore, you should set the bar as high as you possibly can. You are the one who is in charge of your own standards. You don't have to settle for less than what you want from life.

Perhaps the difference between those who reach great heights and those that don't is that the latter weren't able to look up high enough. I am not for one minute suggesting that success is as easy as setting an ambitious goal, but without the VISION, you might as well concede before you start. The vision is the first part of the process. Once the goal has been set, that is when it becomes practical. It becomes about the work and your application of knowledge.

So as we progress through this section of the book, I invite you to start setting the bar high. Set the highest standards for yourself, Aim higher, think bigger, and encourage your unique imagination to guide you.

- How great would you like to look and feel?
- How amazing do you want your relationships to be?
- What level of fulfilment do you want to achieve from your work?
- How much quality do you want in your life?

One thing I can assure you is that in terms of success, you will get what you deserve. Either way. Set the bar high and work hard and you'll get what you deserve. Settle for less and shy away from the work, and you'll get what you deserve.

REMOVE ENTITLEMENT

The moment that you feel you are entitled to something is the moment that the tide turns against you.

Entitlement is a big problem today, especially for the younger generation. With everything being just a click, swipe, or tap away, modern technology has shortened the patience curve.

Nothing is yours until you make it so. You aren't guaranteed to have anything. Not success, not wealth, not even health. It is all fragile and the many forces and factors around you can change at any time. We are all at risk of feeling entitled to things since most of us were raised in conditions consisting of love and nurture. We build our understanding of the world on an emotional level between the ages of 0-7 and so during that time, we are also building up an awareness of what we feel we are entitled to, under the secure protection of our elders.

When we reach adult life, we almost need to undo some of the understanding we have built. As a parent myself, I can see how hard it is to 'get it right'. Don't love enough and there will be issues, love too much and there will be issues. There is no right way of doing things. All we can do is our best and put our own personal dramas to the side to give the next generation the most organic experience possible.

The reality is, when we reach adulthood we have to learn what it all means all over again. We are more directly at threat on a personal level. At this stage, entitlement is a massive weakness.

The sooner we realise that NOTHING is guaranteed, the sooner we are able to take control.

INCREASE YOUR STOCK VALUE

One of the best ways to increase your potential for happiness and success is to increase your own personal stock value. This philosophy applies in all areas of life. Increasing your stock value is all about INVESTING in yourself. There are a number of ways that you can invest in yourself. You can invest MONEY, TIME, AND ENERGY. When you invest in yourself, you get the highest return on investment. You cannot lose an investment that you make in yourself.

If you want better health, a leaner body, or increased performance, you must invest time, energy, and effort in yourself. Increase your stock value with each meal you eat and each workout you complete. If you want better, more exciting and fulfilling relationships, then invest time in yourself for self-care, learn more, broaden your horizons to increase the number of topics you can engage in a conversation with. Make yourself more VALUABLE in an integral sense. By doing so, you will open up more opportunities to engage with people. If you want more money or a different job situation, then make yourself as VALUABLE as you can. Increase your personal skills, your subject expertise, and raise your energy and effort. Show your stock value has increased and then make sure that the relevant conversations happen to discuss how you will be rewarded for your increased value. Money is an energy and is exchanged for your value.

You should always be investing in yourself to raise your stock value. Every experience you have increases it once you are able to change its meaning for a productive one. Even the hardest of challenges bring you value once you identify yourself as a 'survivor.'

The next time you feel frustrated at the lack of results or progress, remember that investing in yourself changes the MOST important variable in any of your situations.

YOU.

INCREASE YOUR CHANCES

Sitting at home on your own rarely increases your chances of success. In order to change your situation, you must be able to disrupt your environment and your current patterns of play. This philosophy is especially prevalent for those who are looking to build stronger, more fulfilling relationships and find love.

One example and a strategy that I always encourage my clients to do is to go for a coffee on your own. Just you and a book. At first, this seems like a scary and non-attractive thing to do! Most people fear that they will look lonely and stick out like a sore thumb! It's actually the complete opposite.

Nobody is going to walk past you while you're in your room at home. So going for a coffee on your own, with a book, and engaging eye contact and smiling at those who look your way simply RADIATES confidence. I can guarantee it will increase your chances of meeting people! This philosophy also applies in other areas of life.

If you are looking to influence decisions in the workplace or get noticed by the decision makers, you must do what you can to raise your chances. Follow them on Twitter and interact with them. Comment on the same posts as they do on LinkedIn. Go to the same places that they do on lunch break. Introduce yourself directly with great energy and eye contact, or if you aren't able to reach them, then introduce yourself to people who can introduce you!

These tips are worthy of a book of their own and there is plenty I can share with you on influence and communication, but for today, just know that sitting still achieves nothing. As soon as the frustration kicks in, ask yourself this question.

- WHAT CAN I DO TO INCREASE MY CHANCES OF SUCCESS?

See if you can come up with at least four answers. These answers become your OPTIONS. Options that you didn't have while you were dwelling on your frustration.

DO WHATEVER IT TAKES

When it comes down to it, the fight inside of you needs to come out.

At some point, it will be necessary for you to take the ultimate BACK YOURSELF stance and be ready to do whatever it takes. This could be working all the hours of the day, travelling miles and miles, being vulnerable, being brave, sending that message, or ultimately doing whatever it is that you must to pull or push yourself forward. It might seem like a case of you versus someone else/other people, but it's almost definitely you versus you.

Be willing to do whatever it takes for as long as it takes to do it. If you want it enough, you'll find the fight.

TAKE RISKS

'Fortune favours the brave.'

This saying has been used in many different cultures to express the same thing. The ones that have a prepared mind, the ones who are bold and the ones who take risks are the ones who receive the greatest amount of fortune. Let's look at these two words, fortune and brave.

What is fortune? The Goddess "Fortuna" is the Goddess of luck. I love this correlation. When it comes to success, luck is not chance. Luck is simply the essence of hard work and opportunity. Luck, opportunities, success, fortune, whatever you call it, is more apparent to those who are 'brave.'

So what does it mean to be brave? Brave is an adjective for one who possesses COURAGE. Courage is necessary in order to take risks, and taking risks is necessary to achieve something extraordinary. After all, it's only labelled as a risk if it's seen as something that is hard, dangerous, rare, or requires sacrifice. We are programmed to avoid such situations.

Our mind simply wants us to stay safe and survive, so it will do whatever it can to sabotage a 'risky move'. Risky moves are required for dreams to become a reality. This is where most people fall short of their dreams and never breakthrough to the level of success they desire. The ones who are able to overcome the risk are able to clearly see the reward. Once the reward outweighs the risk, we are able to logically accept the actions that must take place. Yet still, so many people don't act.

Logical thinking will only get you to the edge, Emotional thinking will allow you to take the leap. The emotion of DESIRE must outweigh the emotions of fear. COURAGE is the catalyst for action and once this equation is implemented, we are able to push through the risk and open up an exciting world of reward.

You have to be ready to take risks. Whether they are big or small, they are required to achieve your full potential. If it were easy, everyone would be living their dream life. NOBODY is successful by accident. Anybody who has ever achieved anything has done so through hard work, courage. and by taking a few risks along the way.

#BackYourselfShare

What risk have you been too scared to take...until now?

MOVE FORWARDS AT ALL TIMES

This is an exceptional core belief.

"Keep moving forwards. That's how winning is done!" One of my favourite lines from one of my favourite movies - the first Rocky. Sylvester Stallone's character was right, that really is how winning is done.

When you simplify things into two possible options, it becomes clear:

1. Stay still
2. Move forwards

You must keep moving forward. Even a small step is a success. This belief can be especially apparent at the end of something you didn't want to conclude. Maybe a relationship, a job, or even someone you love passing away. It's not about moving on, it's about moving forward.

Taking the things that you cannot control or change, accepting them, finding the things you CAN control or change and then moving FORWARDS. For as long as your heart beats you have a choice and as long as you have a choice, it's possible.

BE A VICTOR, NOT A VICTIM

This is a belief that will empower you.

It is not always an easy one to get your head around or to fully accept, but in doing so, you will elevate your position in life to a place of higher health, happiness, and fulfilment. Having a victim mentality will most definitely hold you back from ever moving on, moving forward or indeed moving up in the world. A victim mentality is where one cannot recognize that the person in question OWNS the choice of attitude.

You and I will always control and therefore be able to choose our own attitude. No matter what life throws at us, no matter what happens, we will always own that choice and we CAN choose to be happy. The moment you can evolve your thinking beyond the shortcomings that life has 'given you' is the moment you gain full control over how you feel. There are four key messages I can share with you to help guide your awareness:

- Let go of what you cannot control
- Take charge of what you can control
- You cannot control other people
- You cannot control mortality

Although your voice counts and you can influence the environment around you, there is a large aspect of society, government, and everyday life that you cannot control either. You CAN control your attitude. ATTITUDE is everything.

You can choose to find the opportunity in any situation. You can choose to appreciate and be grateful. You can choose to communicate positively. You can choose the meaning you give to the perceived negativity in your life, including the unforeseen events that have led you to feel negative about yourself and your life.

I am no doctor, but I do have an understanding of the mind and human behaviour. I believe that a depression is the sum of a spiral of negative thoughts. A compound effect of negative self-talk that all stems from a miss-controlled attitude. This negative attitude is almost always traced back to a victim mentality.

The world is not out to get you. You are not hard done by. I know that all of this may seem cliché but it's a deep visceral belief of mine. I learned this myself when Jamie died. I had a choice to be a victim or a victor and despite a few very rare and normal blips along the way, I live as the latter on a macro-level in my life.

I had a choice in my life and you have one in yours. Mine was to be the victim of an unforeseen tragedy. The brother who had his perfect life ripped from him. Or, I could choose to accept and let go of what I cannot control and choose to be a victor. I changed its meaning and chose to live my life to the best I possibly can. That is what I would have wanted Jamie to do should it have been the other way around.

A victim mentality will always hold you back. You'll be dealt a bad hand in life because you will always see things as bad. You'll put responsibility down to external factors, other people, situations, politics, the news, the economy, even the weather!

You have been through hardships in your life. These have given you opportunity to grow and learn. You cannot change the past so it's time to change the present. A victim mentality will only attract more drama and negativity in your life. You will manifest the same recurring patterns of self-sabotage and pain. It's time to graduate your thinking. This is an important belief that I always install into my clients. You aren't a victim. You are a VICTOR.

You are an ingenious survivor of everything you've seen and done. That is who you are. You have lessons in your past that you can learn and apply to create more strength and love. Stop asking 'why me?'. It puts you on the effect side of 'cause and effect'. Control and choice exist on the cause side.

You can accept responsibility and cause your own fortune. You can cause your own positivity and success in life. Instead of asking 'why?' ask yourself 'What can I do?' You are a VICTOR. You have the choice and the opportunity to be happy. You have the control and the responsibility to live as your SUPER SELF. So, tell me, what are YOU going to choose? Lose the victim. Defeat it. It's done. Step in and step up. It is time to take the lead and apply a victor's mindset.

ALWAYS RESPOND VS. REACT

There is a distinct difference between a response and a reaction. Whether it's a negative message on your phone, a stressful situation at work, a post you read on Facebook, something negative in the news, you dropping coffee on yourself, or simply being stuck in traffic... EVERY situation brings a choice to REACT or RESPOND.

No single event or thing that happens comes with a default emotion. WE are the creators of our own emotions by the way that we ATTACH MEANING to things that happen. A traffic jam doesn't produce frustration, anxiety or anger. We produce these feelings as a result of making sense of what's going on around us...in this case, slow traffic, an accident, or a road closure.

Another could be that you realise that you have no control over the situation other than how you FEEL about it and you recognize that anger, stress, and anxiety will not serve you, so you instead choose to take a more relaxed and accepting approach, knowing that every situation holds an opportunity. The ability to see things differently and feel things by CHOICE takes time and practice. It's a mindset that you have to adopt and work on until it becomes your automatic stance in life. One way to help you do this is to tell you about the REACT vs RESPOND rule.

The key habit you will learn here, is to strive to respond as much as possible, rather than react. Doing so, will shape your life into a more positive one. Allow me to explain...

I have been a martial artist for much of my life. It has taught me discipline, patience and self-awareness. I have a 2nd Dan black belt in Tae Kwon Do, a 1st Dan black belt in Japanese Ju Jitsu and I have represented England three times at international level in Sport Ju Jitsu. The reason I tell you this now is because I want you to know that fighting, is much like life itself. Sometimes it hits you. Hard! When it does, you have a choice. To react or respond.

An example of a reaction would be to feel the pain and the shock of being punched in the face and lash out in an attempt to hit back, stand up for yourself, and get some points on the board. The problem with this approach is that it lacks control and is action largely motivated by raw emotion. In most cases fear.

A reaction is a sporadic, emotionally fueled, unpredictable behaviour that often causes negative consequences and more problems as the time passes. When a reaction involves other people, it can be very messy and can lead to relationships breaking down, both in personal life and in professional life.

The only way you come back from being hit in the face (in a fight or in life itself) and to stand any chance of winning is to take the hit, and learn from it quickly. You have to anticipate the next move and respond with your own choice of action.

A response is a calculated, planned, and controlled reply to something that happens in your life, an event that was either predicted or unpredicted. The consequences and the outcomes of a response are often in control of the person responding. It allows the person responding to claim control, composure, and to steer the future in the desired direction.

There are so many moving parts in your life; people, technology, circumstances, unforeseen events, the weather - all unpredictable and capable of shaking things up. It's essential to respond to create your best possible outcome.

Take this example for instance; you're going about your everyday business and everything is going to plan until all of a sudden, out of the blue, you get a message. Perhaps from a partner or a friend. The message rubs you up the wrong way by telling you something you just don't want to hear. Perhaps it brings bad news or something that stresses you out. Or maybe you've become a way for them to vent and offload some of their negative energy. It's possible that this is unintentional and could have had a stressful day themselves!

When this type of energy is brought into your day unexpectedly, it can drag you down and change the flow of your day. Things can go from happy to angry or productive to pointless within seconds. So, here's how to stay in control and practice RESPONDING to life rather than REACTING.

There are three golden rules that you should follow in order to perform at your best and to stay in a positive frame of mind. Never address anything important, sensitive, or that elicits emotion within ten minutes of it happening when you are:

- angry
- hungry
- tired

Adhering to these rules will give you more of an opportunity to think straight, act accordingly, and respond in a way that aligns with your values and creates a positive result. It's not always easy to stay close to these rules, so do your best. The chances are that you are breaking one or more of these rules already, so by being consciously aware of them now, you'll make a positive impact on your results.

As an additional tip, if your event requires a communicated reply, try to keep the control by writing up a reply and sending it to yourself. If it's an email, you can literally send it back to yourself. This will allow you to physically OPEN the email and in doing so, you can put yourself in the other person's shoes and notice how it feels when you open and read it. By doing this, it just changes the dynamics slightly and you're able to make sure that you're responding in the best possible way. Another thing you could do is show or ask someone else what they think. Someone trusted, perhaps a family member or close friend, or somebody at work who is of the same interest as you that you could share the message with in order to get their trusted opinion.

Finally, it is always useful to take ten minutes to think over all of the possible outcomes. Start by thinking about the worst outcomes and then the best outcomes, and then find the outcome you want. Remember, nothing is impossible. Anything can happen and you're in control. Look for the opportunity. Once you know your desired outcome, you can work back to realise what words need to be exchanged from you in order to help the outcome become a reality.

To recap, a response is a much better way to reply and deal with any unpredicted, unexpected, or negative random event that happens in your day. A response is calculated, planned and controlled, whereas a reaction is sporadic, emotionally fueled, chaotic and unpredictable.

Next time you're hit in the face by life, take a RESPONSE approach and steer things back in the right direction. Create a positive outcome and notice the opportunity to CHOOSE – it exists at all times.

OWN YOUR PAST, PRESENT, & FUTURE

Anxiety is the application of fear projected into a future that doesn't yet exist. Time is known to us as the past, present, and the future. We have an understanding of the past based on memory, shared experiences, or through documentation. The past is history. It's chiselled into the stone for all to see.

The present is where choice and attitude exist. We can design our life as we practically apply direction and intention into our actions. The present is art. It is how you apply your paintbrush onto a blank canvas. The reality is that this present moment shares an identical sensory experience to that of this time last week, a year ago, and even on your sixth birthday. We exist in the present.

The future is an idea. It doesn't exist yet and so what we tend to do is overthink and overcomplicate the possible outcomes. When we project fear into the future, we feel anxiety. Fear is generated upon reflection of past experiences that have caused us to raise a 'red flag' in similar situations in order to do ANYTHING to prevent that danger happening again. Anxiety is the way that your ego shows you that red flag by signalling, 'Do not put yourself in that danger again'.

This system has been with humanity for years and evolved with us as we pursue our collective purpose to preserve and reproduce life. Sounds like a great survival system, right? The issue is, your ego doesn't know the difference between a lion coming into your house or a room full of your colleagues waiting to hear you speak at the front of the room. Once that fear is felt, it will do what it can to stop you.

If you know that what you are about to do is something that logically makes sense, then there is no need to let fear get in your way. It is impossible to feel the same anxiety towards something once it is in the past. The past is cement, the future is a blank canvas. The key to overcome situational anxiety is to visualize and imagine how you feel upon the successful completion of the task ahead.

You went to the party and it was great.
You went on the date and they smiled at you the whole time.
You spoke in front of the room and you nailed it.
You gave your BEST and that is all you can possibly do.

So, in order to back yourself and to step outside of your comfort zone, you will need to have an awareness of past, present and future. Ready to draw upon strengths, knowledge, and lessons from the past, design and illustrate your life through the strokes of your present paintbrush, and be able to accept the future doesn't yet exist. Visualize the successful completion of your tasks. Remove the concern and trust that when you live by your values and trust your present self, you will succeed.

USE POSITIVE LANGUAGE

There are a number of words in the English language that cause confusion and a disconnect between what we want and what we end up doing. When we talk to ourselves or others, we use a combination of verbal and non-verbal communication. In this chapter, I am specifically referring to the use of words.

We talk to ourselves all of the time. It may seem strange, but we really do. We use our thoughts to communicate with ourselves via an internal dialogue. Some of this communication is in the forefront of our mind and executes consciously, but the majority is done in the background unconsciously. It's similar to a computer in the sense that there could be multiple programs running but only one occupies the users focus at any one time. When we talk to ourselves and to others, it is important that we use language that is conducive to success and that will help us move forwards rather than limit and hinder us.

Changing something that you do on an autonomous and habitual level can be difficult. When I first started to study the power of language, I had to work really hard in order to make the changes stick. The only way to succeed is to keep concentrating on it, notice and catch yourself out when you use negative language and keep on reinforcing the use of positive language. These very subtle but powerful adaptations to your language will help you create a more positive environment for yourself.

Can't = You haven't learned how to yet.
Don't = What DO you want instead?
Won't = What will you do?
Try = You either do or do not.
Shouldn't = What should you do?
Wouldn't = What would you want?

Couldn't = What could you do?

The key now is to notice yourself using these words and challenge yourself to rephrase your language to create a more honest and positive result. It will take time but you can do it.

GET UP MORE TIMES THAN YOU FALL DOWN

Growing up, I dreamt of becoming a footballer. I would play for hours and hours, pretending to be David Beckham and Ryan Giggs. In my youth, I was good but not exceptional at football. It soon became clear to me that it was highly unlikely I would ever be a premiership footballer. But I REALLY wanted to be a champion. Sport was ingrained into me by both of my parents from an early age and it excited me. I wanted to be good and I wanted to win. I wanted to be a sports star.

As well as football, I did Tae Kwon Do. Again, I wasn't the best in class. At all. I couldn't kick high, I wasn't tough, and I wasn't fast. I was average. Although I did have more desire and motivation in my early adult life after coming back from having a number of years off, I was still average at best.

I had never been interested in competitions. Things started to change in my mid-twenties when I began learning Japanese Ju Jitsu. Something was ignited within me and I had found my warrior's spirit. I wanted to test myself.

My sensei invited me to attend a squad training session for the England Sport Ju Jitsu team. I went along and it was one of the toughest sessions I have ever had. I was so dehydrated and exhausted after three hours of fitness and drills, I couldn't even take off my belt. The result of the session was that I managed to beat the guy that was currently representing England at my weight category.

The phone rang later that week and I was invited to continue attending the squad sessions with a view to competing in the WCJJO world championships in Las Vegas six months later. I had three fights in Las Vegas and I lost them all.

sport ju jitsu, a sport I love. I was losing the final bout up until the last five seconds.

My opponent tried to take me to the ground but I reversed his attack and instinctively managed to use his energy against him to throw him onto his back and claim enough points to sway the fight. I held on tight knowing there were only seconds left and then the buzzer went. I knew I had won.

When the judges made the call, my supporters rushed onto the mat and lifted me up. I punched the air and then consulted my courageous opponent, before breaking down in tears on my coach's shoulder. "I knew I could do it," I said.

"So, did I," he replied.

It was a major release.

In 2014, I was crowned the WCJJO Lightweight champion of the world in sport ju jitsu. It is the ultimate result of manifestation. I created the opportunity to represent my country. I said YES. I tasted it and got served defeat. I worked hard to make myself better and then I used every margin I had to squeeze out a win in the last five seconds of a final. It all counts.

I now have the championship belt on a shelf in my office along with the framed England uniform and my medals. It reminds me that we can achieve things we once imagined as impossible when we aim big and keep our focus. I invite you to aim big today and never give up. Get up more times than you fall down.

YOUR GREATEST OPPORTUNITY

We have evolved our consciousness over thousands of years to occupy ambition and desire above and beyond the simplicity of survival. I know that you are the type of person who has an intention to improve. I know this simply because you are reading this book.

The nature of this book is to help you live a happy, healthy, and confident life. The variable that makes all of this important is our mortality. If you knew that you and everyone you care about will live forever, there would be very little urgency for change. The fact is, we are all going to die one day.

It is a simple paradigm that you must be comfortable with thinking about and facing. Mortality is our reminder that time is ticking and that we must act on our ambition in order to live that healthy, happy, and confident life. Positively influencing everyone and everything around us in a way that fits with our life's design and desire.

We fly close to death a number of times in our life before eventually arriving when it is our time. This is something that we should all embrace and use as motivation. When I was younger, I used to cry at night because 'I didn't want to die.' I would have been around eight years old and my concept of life and death had been established, along with the fear of dying. Today, I don't fear death. I believe that this is one of the reasons why I am able to live with courage and in harmony with my purpose. I live in truth and I keep my priorities in line with my STRONGEST REASON WHY.

If I had died today and was able to look down at life, I would feel hard done by that I wouldn't get to be with my family anymore but that would literally last five seconds before I would be GRATEFUL to have had the time I did with them.

When you live life in the essence of opportunity and you are literally doing everything you can with what you've got, it is impossible to regret. When you approach life as the ultimate opportunity, it changes the narrative of your life. You say yes more than you say no and you prioritise your energy, It's time to embrace the greatest opportunity of them all. The fact that you are ALIVE. We cannot control when we die, but we can control how we live. Existing isn't living.

TIME IS THE CURRENCY OF LIFE

Time is the one thing that we all share equally and that nobody can control. It is impossible to have more or less time than anybody else, yet so many people wish for more, or seem to have 'no time' to do what they need and want to do.

The way it changes from person to person is in HOW we spend it. Time is the currency of life. We each have an unknown allocation to spend on the people, tasks, projects and processes that we choose. The key belief here is to take OWNERSHIP of your time. You are the one who controls your spend.

It may be that there are people in your life who are taking way more of your currency than they deserve. Perhaps they lack reciprocity and aren't 'paying' you back evenly. Perhaps there are tasks, projects, or processes that are wasting your currency, causing you to be time-poor with little return to show for it. It is literally 'life money' and just like any currency it can be traded, exchanged, spent, and saved.

If we simply exist and go with the flow in life, we will end up being a resource of economy for other people. In other words, we get used and owned to benefit other people. We MUST take control and take charge of HOW we spend our time. What or who deserves less of your time (or perhaps needs to give you more of theirs to balance your account?) What or who deserves MORE of your time in order to be healthy, happy, and successful?

The only way to change your situation is to first become aware of it, then take responsibility and control of it, before having the courage to change the outcome through calculated action. It is time to be more economical with your life's currency. It's your time. You spend it wisely.

OWN YOUR STRONGEST REASON WHY

This is the most effective and most powerful question you can ask yourself to stay focused and to live as close to your values as possible. Your values are like a code of conduct you have chosen to live your life by. Perhaps you have chosen family, honesty, passion, love, and helping others, for example.

Whatever your values are, their clarity and power can be harnessed and laser focused on a task or project by asking yourself what you 'strongest reason why' really is. The answer will give you the edge you need to power through challenge and distraction. It will allow you to win the battle of intention and to overcome the pull of other people's agendas.

A person who knows and operates on their strongest reason why is a force to be reckoned with. They have resilience, determination, and a warrior spirit. You can be that person everyday by knowing the following:

What is your STRONGEST reason why you are alive?

What is your strongest reason why you want to succeed in your next upcoming task today?

This gives us a macro-sized focus that we can bind our life to - a 'purpose'.

As well as situational motivation to succeed no matter what, applied to every task in your day.

I will help you to think about your strongest reason why by sharing mine with you. My STRONGEST reason why (macro-life):

I am ALIVE. I am here right now, living and breathing. I have a legacy in my son, love in my heart, and time in my hands. For every moment I am here I will strive to make a difference with my opportunity of life.

My strongest reason why (micro-task):

To finish this chapter and make sure I illustrate this point as clearly and concisely as I can in order to help you, the reader, to win your day and evaluate your vision I'm going to tell you a story. I had always known about the concept of 'strongest reason why' but I didn't FULLY understand it until I was coached through it by an incredible mentor of mine Matt Elwell. The lesson came in the last hour of a working day spent at my office planning for my first Super Self Summit.

Matt asked me "what's your strongest reason why?" He called me out and I answered him with 'Legacy.' He challenged me to think deeper. He showed me how I had already achieved a legacy. My son Lincoln is a walking, talking, bundle of joy and legacy. My DNA. Here to outlive my physical time spent on this planet as Tommy Gentleman.

I had been hustling for legacy but already had it. It took me a while to figure it all out. I had realized that I had lost contact with my deeper vision. I was saying things that I thought I should say, instead of really looking inside and taking the time to answer. I had lost touch with the LOVE that is required in all that is to be done. Every task, every human being and every process. Every once in a while, we have to stop and access where we are at and ask questions. Often, it takes somebody else to come in and help us on our orbit. It is impossible to see your own blind spots, and so I hope that I have been able to help you think about it a little deeper today.

Don't just echo buzz-words. Instead, speak your truth. YOUR truth. It's the best (and only) way to orbit as you.

#BackYourselfShare

How can you use the back yourself beliefs to inspire change in your life? What are you going to do differently today versus yesterday? Share a post or a picture to express your positive intentions to the Back Yourself community!

It was a disaster. My inexperience showed as I got my ass kicked and even got disqualified due to being so naïve to the competitive environment. The experience was tough but powerful. I came back to the UK with a choice. Either call it a day and be happy with the fact that I had represented my country at a sport I love. Or, train my ass off and do better in two years time.

I kept going along to sessions and started attending the squad sessions again. I started winning more and more bouts and found myself fast becoming one of the better fighters in the whole team. The news came through that the next world championships would be held in the UK and due to facility availability and logistics, it would be held in my hometown. No brainer. I worked hard and stayed focused. The event came around and I felt good. I went into my fights with confidence and ready to put right what went wrong in Las Vegas. I beat my first opponent easily. Ironically from the USA.

I then went on to beat a handy opponent from Canada before facing a fellow team mate of mine in the final. I can remember thinking to myself, 'well whatever happens now, you've got a medal'. But that wasn't enough for me. Not that day.

The fight was so close. I lost the first round, then won the second. The third and final round ended as a draw! That meant that the result would be decided in overtime. Thirty seconds of free fighting, whoever has the most points at the end wins.

I was up against it, tired, feeling it physically, mentally and emotionally. I remember looking into my opponents' eyes and considering settling for second. Instead, I dug in. I was thirty seconds away from achieving something that I may never get a chance to achieve again. I could be a WORLD CHAMPION in

PART FOUR

Head, Heart, & Hands: Getting Results

THE CONCEPT

I have found that the three biggest barriers that block us from achieving our goals are:

1. Your own ego (in your head)
2. Fear (in your heart)
3. Procrastination (in your hands)

That is why it is important to learn how to connect these three important areas and become a strong force of inspiration, confidence and action. In this chapter, I will break down each area and show you how to bring them all together to remove friction and create a path of least resistance, all the way to success.

YOUR HEAD

Everything starts as an idea first. Inspiration can come from many places. It could be consciously picked up into our awareness through our five senses, or it could be unconsciously received through the deeper cognitions of our mind. Our minds can create a picture of success relatively quickly and easily. Imagination doesn't abide by the laws of space and time. It is possible to create an idea, a vision or an inspired plan in a matter of seconds - one that is highly attractive, exciting and limitless. This is one of our many blessings that we hold as human beings, the ability to create.

So, if it is easy and simple to create a vision or plan of greatness, why is it then that so many people fail to follow through on their ideas? Why is it that something can seem so highly attractive, beneficial and even essential to a happy life, yet NEVER get followed up on? Why is it that even the most logical ideas still fall short, despite someone having heaps of desire to make it happen? Enter, THE EGO. Your ego is like the ultimate defence mechanism that exists in your mind to keep you safe.

Human beings have evolved over thousands of years and the ego has evolved with us. Its main job is to keep you safe, but it doesn't understand the TASK. Your ego can't recognise the difference between modern day tasks that may bring about anxiety such as speaking in public, asking someone out on a date, going to a new exercise class, or indeed primitive threats to your existence such as the threat of being eaten by a predator. It is built and developed throughout your life to help you avoid situations that may cause you upset, distress, annoyance, trauma, and/or despair. It would rather you feel the pain that you've felt before, a pain that you already know, rather than risk going into the unknown, and potentially facing worse pain.

Your ego doesn't understand that you have ambition and want to create a better future. It doesn't see the reward, only the risk. People sometimes mistake the ego for something that's chauvinistic, or arrogant. They'll say things like, 'That's just his ego talking, or he's so egotistic.' But really, what they're referring to in these instances, are behaviour patterns that display confidence in a situation where the person backs themselves 100%. An action, behaviour, or situation that they know they're good at.

Now if you know that you're good at something, you'll naturally want to show it off. You'll want to express yourself because you have both proven confidence and competence. If your ego understands that you're good at something, and by doing it, you're going to attract positive attention to yourself, it will happily move out of the way and let you proceed. It won't if it thinks you'll be in danger or if it brings up feelings of fear you may have been stung by in the past, such as fear of rejection, failure, or of looking stupid.

Let's take an example, of somebody who is very good at dancing. They would always take the opportunity to dance and soon gain a reputation of being the person who's always busting a move. Some people might think that it is egotistic to always be showing off moves in public whenever presented with the opportunity to do so. Let's say this same person was presented with an opportunity to do karaoke, but they knew that they weren't that confident with their own vocal talents and that there could be a risk of being laughed at or feeling embarrassed should they put themselves in that situation. If they chose to avoid taking part based on these fears, it would have been their ego that intercepted the opportunity to say, 'you're a terrible singer, you'll make a fool of yourself, stay away!'

The ego will simply step in and say no because it understands there's a risk of looking stupid. Your ego will back what it already knows. It would rather you do nothing than risk being embarrassed, to look stupid, or to be in a position that is unsafe, or insecure. Confidence and courage will give you the power to battle against your own ego, and recognise the reward really does outweigh the risk. For example, the reward could be something health based. Perhaps, you have a goal of what you'd like your body to look like, or what size clothing you'd like to wear. The vision exists in your mind, and in order to carry out the actions required to make them a reality, you must apply confidence and courage to help override your ego, which wants you to stay the same until convinced otherwise.

Remember, it would rather play it safe, and keep things the same. Your ego will increase the volume of doubt if it feels that is what is required to stop you from stepping into the unknown. Your ego will tell you the story it needs tell you, to keep you stuck in the same place. Its voice will be the loudest unless you have something that is even stronger in the form of confidence and courage.

Sometimes, we can feel a powerful wave of confidence and courage, apply some action and start doing something, only to be pulled right back to square one like a big elastic band. I call it the 'ego elastic'. It is a real thing and it hits a lot of people. It's very common in a health and fitness environment. Take for instance, someone who wants to get in shape, joins a gym, turns up every day for two weeks, really sticks to the plan, but then falls off the wagon.

It's the ego that makes this happen, by taking into consideration the challenges presented such as lack of time, too busy, not enough energy, results are too slow etc., and the ego says 'It's OK, just go back to how things were, it wasn't that bad, and you don't really need to go to the gym anyway. Just relax.'

When really, it is something they want for themselves and would greatly benefit the individual. It takes courage to cut that ego elastic. The way to do it is to BACK YOURSELF based on the inner strength that you have gained through life, amplified by a STRONG reason why you want the outcome. That is why we need LOVE to help cut that ego elastic.

nobody suffers as a result of your actions, whereas people who are motivated by the mind alone, can sometimes put other people down in the process of them succeeding.

Love is essential and especially where we wish to be better and push ourselves. We can very easily neglect the importance of love. It has many different levels and many different forms, but love is essentially life and it exists in the heart. Love overcomes fear, and fear will always hold you back.

Fear causes anxiety. Anxiety is simply the fear from past experiences, projected onto a possible future outcome that doesn't exist yet. Fear belongs in the past. Fear presents itself in many different ways. Fearful situations can vary from person to person, and it all depends on life experience. Fear is learnt, none of us are born with fear (well, other than the fear of falling, although I would argue that was a response rather than a fear.) So we are born fearless and pick things up as we go. Fear can cripple future plans, and when it's combined with that overprotective ego you get stuck. Whenever we feel anxiety towards something, it's because we haven't yet crossed the line of fear.

Combining the love with the great ideas that you have in your mind, will help you to build enough energy around the tasks that have to happen in order for you to conquer the fear and move forwards. This is where the hands come into play.

YOUR HANDS

The hands are what cause the action to occur. Without the action, all you've got are great ideas, inspiration, and the thought of what might be. It's the hands that make it happen. It's the hands that cause things to change. So many people have ideas, they have a plan, they have desire, and they have all the best intentions coming from a great space of positivity and intent but they don't do anything about it.

Procrastination is the enemy of the hands. Procrastination is where we do nothing but we know we should do something. It's not a great place to be, we always feel like we're failing because deep down we either know we should be doing more, or we know we should be doing something better with our time. Procrastination is completing an entire series on Netflix, instead of replying to those emails. Without the hands, nothing gets done and you'll risk living in regret.

True success in the face of challenge will only occur when the head, heart, and hands connect. This is how to create an abundance of health, happiness, and success in your life. Ideas and inspiration are created in the head. Our strongest reason why, amplified by love from our heart, can help override the ego. The hands take action and sculpt our reality into a happy and successful one.

Remember, it can be tough out there, but you have to fight for what you believe you can do and what is important to you. Happiness is there for you and when it's linked to your ambition, things can get complicated, so get to it by using your head, heart and hands.

Back Yourself Share **#BackYourselfShare**

What's the number one action you will take TODAY to move closer to your goals? Share with the Back Yourself community so I can see what you're going to do and you can stay accountable!

PART FIVE

You & Your People

CARE FOR YOUR PHYSICAL BODY

Exercise is important. I know that you know this. In fact, I would go as far as to say that every single human being on planet earth recognises the value of exercise one way or another, either consciously or unconsciously.

Exercise is connected to feeling and looking your best. It is considered the solution for low body confidence and being out of shape. Exercise is also considered an area which a lot of people struggle with. They struggle to keep their momentum, to do the right exercise, and more often than not, to do it at all.

Your body is designed to move. You are supposed to express your human movement. It is part of your gift and your purpose. Throughout the history of humanity, we have embraced our human potential to help us survive and express ourselves. To hunt food, escape danger, jump, climb, swim, swing, and stretch. As humans, we have always held a strong need to belong as a part of a group. It's a survival instinct we all have deep inside.

In the modern world, we approach exercise as a method to maintain health, enjoy activities, achieve personal milestones, experience new things and express our unique identity. Unfortunately, exercise has also become something that is surrounded by expectation, comparison, and anxiety. It's something we all know is good for us, necessary for health and something we all need, yet DOING it can often be intimidating, confusing and even traumatic.

Whether that's based on negative experiences in P.E. at school, or the pressures of society to 'look' a certain way, exercise can get a bad press in adulthood. Starting a new exercise regime can challenge your identity. It can dig up old hurt if we attach it to embarrassment, discomfort, and insignificance that we may have felt around exercise in the past.

As we grow and get older, we start to cement our identity within society. If you are somebody who doesn't exercise, the longer you leave it, the more fixed you'll become in that understanding of your identity, and the harder it becomes to CHANGE. In the same way, people who exercise regularly will create an identity, understood by themselves and those around them, as somebody who trains.

Starting an exercise regime requires a level of vulnerability and acceptance. You are faced with JUDGEMENT from other people and by yourself. It provokes fear of rejection and can touch on sensitive patterns experienced in the past. Past failures, past embarrassment, and possibly even past negative judgement. Whether you exercise on a regular basis or not, today, I urge you to move the judgement of yourself and other people to the side, overcome your own ego, and accept that the BEST version of you is a healthy and energetic person; a person who embraces exercise on a regular basis.

The first thing to consider when it comes to regular exercise is that you move your body in a safe and effective way. Every single body is different. I would strongly recommend before you start anything new, or if you've not exercised in the last three months, that you visit your GP to make sure that you are ready and able to safely start a new exercise regime. I have to say that because it's my responsibility to make sure you do this safely and effectively.

Your body can move in an exceptional number of ways, and you've got to make sure what you do is safe and effective. The best combination for results when it comes to regular exercise is to do a combination of strength training, cardiovascular exercise, flexibility exercises and stretches, and the secret ingredient, make it fun. You've got to treat your body with the utmost respect and care. You've only got one body, one vessel of life, and so make sure you exercise on a regular basis to ensure you are maintaining for the best possible life it can have.

You owe it to yourself to show up as the best physical representation of yourself, and to do that, exercise is a central ingredient. It's good for your heart, your lungs, your muscles, your joints, your skeletal system, and your nervous system. It releases endorphins, helps you combat stress, raises your confidence, reduces your body fat, and improves your overall health.

YOUR HEART

Love can be the courage that you need. Love is the centre of everything. Originally, when I first started talking on stage about the head and the heart, it was all about ensuring that love was present in everything you do, and the reasons why you do it.

My presentation emphasised that you should love the process, love the people, and love the purpose. Love is an essential ingredient for success no matter what it is you're doing. To do things powered by the ideas in your head and in the absence of love causes a problem later down the line.

For me, it was about constantly telling myself I wasn't good enough, and therefore always looking to achieve more, and motivating myself to succeed, but never allowing myself to feel the benefit, reward, satisfaction, and pride in my achievements. For almost two years, I kept my head down, drove it hard and didn't take any time to stop, step back, and enjoy my success. I made myself numb to success.

I'd always want to do something else because I still felt like I wasn't good enough. I'd beat myself up about my situation, thinking that was a good way of motivating myself. I found myself constantly comparing myself to other people and focusing on the things I didn't have, instead of the things I did have.

I'd lost gratitude and I had lost the love for my circumstances. I had an idea of love, but I didn't understand it's real power when it comes to loving the process and the journey. When you fire up from a place of love, everything improves. The lefts, the rights, the up, the downs, the ins, and the outs figure themselves out much quicker and with less drama when you fire up from a place of love. Relationships will always be integral. With love,

LOVE STARTS WITH YOUR 'SELF'

Relationships. They are about love, they are about connecting with other human beings and guess what, it all starts with you. We have an inbuilt primal drive to seek other people we like and that are like us. It is in our DNA as human beings. If we are on our own, we are isolated. We are at risk of living under stress and pressure that goes against our survival needs, as a human being. That's why we're always stronger in groups.

These groups can show up in different ways in the modern world. They could be your tight family unit, the ones who you have known all your life. They could be a group of friends you do something with on a regular basis, maybe known as the 'guys" or 'girls'. It could be the people you hang out with at the weekend, go watch a rugby or football match with, or the group of friends you catch up with at the local coffee shop. It could also be the people you go to an exercise class with, your work colleagues, people you interact with every day. Perhaps it's someone you share an interest with, like a fan club, a brand that you have identified with, or some other kind of club that meets on a regular basis to discuss similar interests.

Relationships are built on shared values, morals, and beliefs. When a relationship breaks down, it's when one or more of the people's values, morals, and beliefs have changed. Either through their actions or through their own thoughts and feelings. The golden rule in relationships is that you can never change anybody else. We've all got free will, we are born with it and it never stops growing, unless you stop it from growing. We learn to use it as we go through childhood and into our teenage years; until we eventually become an adult and fully fend for ourselves. Everything starts with you!

As hard as it may seem, you shouldn't depend on other people for love. Raise your levels of self-love and you'll attract more love in your life. It is impossible to know what anybody else is thinking. People are complicated. Things change and evolve and people will come in and out of your life.

Nobody likes to be rejected, nobody likes to be dumped or ditched, but if it was to happen, YOU need to be okay with yourself. You need to be able to add love into your own tank instead of relying on other people to fill it up for you. Yes, life is better when we are part of a group, and yes, life is better when we are in a shared, intimate relationship. The quality of your relationships will directly reflect your relationship with yourself. We are happiest when we have friends or family who we regularly bounce positive energy with. But, at the end of the day, everything is a reflection of your own self-love and respect. Imagine the relationship with another person as a frequency.

Have you ever said, that someone was on the same wavelength as you? Or that you like someone's 'vibe'? We all like people who are like ourselves. Some of this recognition is an obvious conscious observation, such as noticing that you like the same things, dress similarly, or follow the same team. Other aspects are unconsciously processed. We read each other's body language within microseconds and instantly form an opinion of each other based on an intuitive thought process. We attract people who are on the same frequency as us. Low-frequency relationships are attracted into your life when you think badly of yourself and have a low self-worth. When you don't respect yourself as much as you should, you'll attract people who don't respect you as much as they should.

Over the last few years, I have worked with many of my clients to help them through rocky relationships. When a relationship starts to break down and fracture, it is usually down to the fact that one or both of the people involved have changed frequency either up or down. This disturbs the understanding between the two people. It alters the energy and humans are always in a constant exchange of energy.

Perhaps, a relationship was established when one of the people were in a place of vulnerability, sadness, hurt, fear, doubt, or guilt. These emotions are strong vibrations that appeal to other people who have similar scale insecurities. Insecurity is fear of rejection, low confidence, low self-esteem and ultimately low levels of self-love. It will disrupt the ability to grow or evolve a relationship.

The change of direction in a relationship can occur when one person in the relationship has increases in self-belief and self-worth, causing a resistance against certain behaviours that are no longer tolerated. The first person may choose to ignore or give less to the other person, in an 'I am not putting up with this anymore' type attitude. This changes the energy in the relationship and doing so could make person two feel they need more attention and energy. Sometimes, the way people act to draw in more attention and energy is to run their familiar drama patterns. To the weaker of us, it could show up as destructive and negative behaviour. Behaviour that could potentially end the relationship or at least cause a bust up.

Your vibe attracts your tribe and that is true for all relationships. Sometimes, we need to be strong enough to have a crunchy conversation to help things move forwards. Attention seeking is a very real thing. Human beings exchange and trade energy all of the time and some people need more than others.

If we're in a negative place, we will attract people who match that frequency. We will also attract those who thrive off of negativity.

And so, if we don't love and respect ourselves, we will eventually attract people who don't love and respect us. Instead, they will abuse that relationship. They will abuse our trust, abuse our vulnerability, and they will end up stealing energy from us in order to better themselves. Our relationships should be a shared identity. This goes with relationships on an intimate level and also with friends, colleagues, and family. For it to work, you must first share an identity of values, morals, and beliefs.

I love working with a single client looking to meet someone and build a loving relationship. We were put here to find and feel love between one another. Much like you and I, they are ultimately looking to fall in love with someone who they enjoy spending time with. More often than not, these types of clients have had relationships in the past that have broken down, and now they've taken themselves to a better place where their own levels of self-care, self-worth, self-belief, and self-love have increased. When that happens, it's an amazing thing. They find someone without even looking, because people are attracted to the same frequency, and they have changed theirs.

As I said, treat yourself badly, you'll attract bad relationships. Treat yourself with care and love, and that goes right from your food choices to what you do and think behind closed doors when no one's looking. You will attract someone who has the same level of care and love for you. The same goes for your friendship circle.

One of the most common questions I get asked is, 'How can I get my partner to think this or feel that?' Now, influence is a real thing. We can influence people to alter their perception and, therefore, give them the potential to change, but we can never control anybody else. Just like everything starts with YOU, everything for them, starts with THEM. It really is the golden rule. It has to start with you! Knowing your standards of what's appropriate and acceptable for your life; and never compromising on those standards is a great rule to have. You cannot change anyone else. The things they do to you, the way they make you feel will often be a reflection of how they feel about themselves.

We're all connected as human beings, but we decide and choose to share our lives with certain people, who we feel a deep belonging with. You always have a choice. Either help and influence a relationship to a better frequency and a more positive place, or simply let that person go on their own journey, whilst you go on yours.

This takes a level of courage, but that courage comes when you are loving towards yourself. You should always love yourself before you start to exchange love with someone else. The more self-love you feel, the greater the depth of confidence and self-worth, and therefore less insecurity and more love you will have to trade with someone. You might think you don't love yourself, but you do. I know you do because you're reading this book right now. That means you care enough about your well-being, that you want to be happy and healthy. You are seeking information to feel better and do more in the form of self-development and that is self-love.

I know you've got dreams, ambitions, and aspirations, and that is deep at your core. You do want to live a fulfilled and satisfied life. That is perfectly fine and should be harnessed in an honest and integral way. The meaning of life is to find happiness and love. Embracing this is also a form of self-love, in the shape of positive desire.

At the time of writing this book, I watched 'The Greatest Showman' with Hugh Jackman and Zac Efron. The famous line in that film is, "Everything you ever want, everything you ever need, is right there in front of you." This is especially powerful when you are stood in front of a mirror. You have to be okay with looking at your own reflection. It pains me that there are so many people out there that won't look at theirs in the mirror because they're ashamed, or they feel guilty, or they feel hurt or sad, and these negative emotions are showing up in multiple occasions in their everyday life.

This will manifest into self-harm in the form of mental or emotional abuse. We put ourselves down and think we aren't good enough. This deep void of insecurity requires a consistent top up of energy. Attention that we seek from other people. We look to fill that tank of energy, and we behave in a way that seeks this attention from others. This can often show up in a really negative way, trapping us in negative loops of false expression, fake smiles, and often depression.

I'm not saying you have to look in the mirror and flood yourself with a ton of compliments repeating, 'I am INCREDIBLE', but actually, it would help! There's a difference between confidence and arrogance, and we'll talk about that when we get to the confidence section of the book. For now, what I want you to understand is that you must be okay with looking in the mirror. You ARE an incredible person. You're a human being that is here and alive right now. That's a miracle.

You are the only person who will ever be you in the history of the whole universe. Everything that you understand, everything you don't, everything that exists around you, all of it, you are the only person that will ever be you. That's a special gift. You owe it to yourself to fall in love with you. You're amazing...

Relationships are the flavour of fun in our lives. The people we share moments and memories with, make it all worthwhile as we pull together for a common cause of 'leaving this planet a better place than what we found it'. We all have a single legacy to live, a purpose, a destiny, something that is there for us, as a 'yet to be fulfilled duty' to mankind.

You've got a job to do while you're alive on this planet. Live in a state of happiness, and have meaningful, positive, loving relationships with other people that help them and you smile more. I call it the sweet-spot of happiness. You can become a beacon of light and energy for other people, by simply turning that light on within yourself and realising it's okay to be a 'work in progress'. It's okay to want things you haven't quite got yet. It is also essential you understand what you already have which is the beautiful gift of life itself.

You really are an amazing person who deserves to feel good. Everything you've ever been through in your life has made you who you are today. That's a powerful gift. You're here and you're alive, and you have the opportunity to connect with other people.

Successful relationships are key to a wider success in life. As human beings, the way we attract other people, and the groups that we belong in, and our social needs and desires, all form a part of who we are as a person.

People are an integral part of the journey. Every goal you have will include a relationship element to it. Whether it be your body, your work situation, or your overall success, it will be necessary to have strong, loving, and reciprocal relationships around you. Of course, we should be supportive but not at the expense of our own life enjoyment and experience. You are not a harvest of energy that's there to be feasted on by other people to suit their selfish agenda.

Jim Rohn, famously said, "We are the average of the five people we spend the most time with." meaning, we are a mirror of these people. So, who do you spend your time with right now? Is there a negative person in your life who drags you down and always seems to have a problem? Perhaps someone who steals your energy and seems to enjoy drama? If so, consider spending less time with that person. They will negatively influence you and drop your frequency. I'm not saying that you should cut them off completely. What I am saying is you should take charge of the relationship, and how much time and energy they take from you. Snap out of the pattern and get out of their agenda. Start to take control of your own time and energy. You can fill the void with people who respect you, inspire you, encourage you, support you, and guide you unconditionally. At the end of the day; human beings exchange energy with each other.

Sometimes people steal a little bit more than what they deserve because they are lacking in something. You are a human being designed to interact and trade energy in a fair way so that both people can smile, and win. That is our goal and our purpose, it is why we exist. To better the conditions of this planet by simply loving ourselves and each other equally and allowing that love to flow. There is too much at stake. This is your life, and you deserve to be happy. Remember, that in all relationships that exist in your life, YOU have the power to improve them.

It all starts with YOU. It has to, you are the one who has evolved your level of understanding, self-development, and courage. Overcome your own insecurities. Express yourself. Speak your truth and don't hold back.

COMMUNICATE BETTER WITH THE PEOPLE IN YOUR LIFE

The way that we communicate with our fellow human beings will determine the quality of our relationships. We can have three different classes of relationship:

- intimate relationships
- friends and family
- everybody else in the world

We have to look at the ways in which we communicate within these three classes and we need to understand the best strategies for harbouring healthy and happy relationships.

Firstly, let's approach the intimate relationship in your life. By the way, if this position is currently vacant, that's ok! What you are about to learn will help you to form and maintain a healthy intimate relationship when the right person comes along!

- How often do you communicate with your partner in a high-quality fashion?
- How often do you sit down and talk about your goals?
- When was the last time you discussed your shared vision?
- How often do you share what's really going on in your life?

All of the above are examples of the level of meaning and depth that all intimate relationships deserve and demand. Time is the currency of life. It is ours to spend and our partner deserves to have the best of us. In this fast-paced world we live in, it can be very difficult for us to achieve this flow of quality time. Quality time is so important for people when it comes to an intimate relationship. I can literally feel when my relationship with my wife Kelly is starting to get stressful and I know it's time to step in and create some quality time to communicate.

We may do this by going out for dinner, sitting opposite each other with our phones off, letting the conversation flow naturally and organically. Sometimes, we might do a more practical and planned strategic catch up where we communicate on our goals and we make sure we understand where each other is coming from. We help each other to understand the demands, stresses, and concerns that we have in our head, thus allowing each other to understand why behaviour patterns may be different to how they usually are. We also share triumphs and successes to make sure we can celebrate together! This style of support is just as important as being there in hard times.

Quality communication prevents confusion and builds shared confidence. It is vital to share your journey with your partner. Not only do you need the support of the person closest to you, but you also want to build trust and eliminate anxiety. This is especially important when you want to start doing something new. Whether it is starting a new course, a new habit, a new hobby, or wanting to try something different, you must involve your partner and help them understand your reason why. When your partner doesn't understand, it can become a big problem. Assumptions start and past drama patterns can grow into insecurities.

I see this a lot with my clients, especially in the early stages of our work together. There becomes a point where all of the new habits and changes start to alarm the radar of their partner. The partner starts to worry and fear the change, and in their actions, start to sabotage the progress and the journey. Sometimes, it's conscious and on purpose, but most of the time it's unconscious and done without realising. They may become concerned that they aren't good enough anymore and their insecurities grow.

Quality communication solves this. What's really important to realise with this particular section of is that the person we're talking about here is your partner, the person you love, the person you want to spend your life with. At least that's what I hope.

At this stage in the book, perhaps it's a chance for us to really reflect on the power of an intimate relationship. Ask yourself...if this is as good as it gets, is it good enough? Now, if your answer to that is no, then you've got to spend some considerable amount of time thinking about what you deserve and what you want in life. Communication is essential with the people in our lives on an intimate level, and again, everything starts with you, so communicate with yourself and figure out:

- Is this something you actually want?
- Is it something you want to fight for?
- Is this something you want to grow and nurture?

Consider this deeply and providing all of the above are affirmative, let us move on. It is important to remain open and to be a great listener. After all, it works both ways. Learn to recognise the signs your partner gives to you when they need to sit down and confide in you.

Nobody is a mind reader.
I'll repeat.
Nobody is a mind reader.
We will not get the hints.

Ladies and Gents, your partner will not get the hints that you give them! The drama patterns you project onto your partner – such as playing the sympathy card or over exaggerating your efforts in a bid to 'receive a medal' – is unnecessary and lacks emotional maturity. Behaving in a way that is seeking attention is not the way in which you create quality communication. The way you create quality communication is you don't wait for it, you create it yourself. You create it yourself and at the same time you keep an open eye on the behaviour, the words, and the actions of your partner to recognise when they're acting out of character. Learn to know when they seem a bit down, when their frequency and energy is lower than normal, and when physical contact starts to be less frequent. This is when YOU have to be the one to step in and create some communication to bind and build.

Always remember, this person should be someone you trust and are open with. It's fine to get straight to the point. It's okay to say you're not okay and it's alright to support and give everything that you've got and be vulnerable with this person in your life. Second to yourself, this person is the one who you share the most of your love with.

At first, you love yourself and then you share that love with somebody else. The love you give them, they reciprocate with love they give to you, in turn topping up your love levels through whatever it is that does it for you. Here are the ways people feel most loved:

- physical contact
- material things
- spending quality time with you
- doing nice things for you
- simply telling you how great you are

Figure out which of those five things you need from your partner. Which one helps you feel most loved? Which one do you think makes your partner feel most loved? Perhaps you could even ask them.

Everybody is different and what we need to realise is that our way of doing things might not be the same as theirs. Relationships on the intimate level are about give and receive. We have to give without expectation and allow the receiving to happen organically. It's a shared identity between two people that still have their own identity.

Communication is also very important when it comes to your close friends and family. Some of your friendships are timeless, the type of connections that always seem to take off from where you last left it, no matter how long it has been. For me, it's 'my boys', the group of friends I went to school with. I am grateful I still hang out with the majority of them, even now, fourteen years after leaving school. I've kept a core group of friends because we share the same values, morals and beliefs, and anyone who dipped in and out of the friend group has either changed their morals, values, or beliefs, or no longer align with ours as a group.

Ultimately, that's what it comes down to. Communication is what keeps these relationships alive. Even the ones which you just click back into still need a bit of love and attention. When it comes to a friend group, we've all got our own identity in a way that we slot in to and the way that we fit in what's expected with each other. I guess one person has to have the responsibility of sending that message or making that phone call and why shouldn't that person be you?

It has to be someone, and who better to do it than the one that takes pride in their own personal development by reading books like this one? When was the last time you saw your best friend? When did you last go out and spent time with your tribe? Perhaps, it's time to do that again or at least get something in the diary. We need this, from a primal perspective we have to belong to groups. It's what gives us a sense of social security and increases the chances of survival through strength in numbers and the pack-like mentality.

Sometimes, we can let our intimate relationships dominate all of our time and we have little time left to spend with our tribe, but it's so important that we still get it. I'd recommend joining a club or some kind of organisation that gets you out of the house on a routine basis. Do things that can bring a different element and flavour of relationship into your life. Communication has to start somewhere, so why not start with you?

Finally, communication with everybody else in the world. Whether that is people on the street or on social media, it's quite simple; you attract what you project in life. When you walk down the street, you're bringing a certain flavour, a certain energy, a certain vibe into the universe. Simply smiling at someone starts a ripple effect of positivity. You will start to become that beacon of light to others. You will give off a 'vibe' that people will pick up on. Sometimes, it will be an obvious observation and other times it will be a subtle subconscious energy that is attractive to other people.

I like to practice a smile that doesn't feel silly or over the top. For me, it's lips pursed together, smile wide, no teeth showing. Sounds mad doesn't it?! But it is a strategy that I choose to use to give off energy to those around me. Try it. You'll be surprised at how many people say hello, nod, or indeed smile back. Some people might ignore you. That's still very possible, but that's more about them than it is about you. At least you've done what you can to spread the positivity.

Social media is still communication. You communicate with the world around you, every time you put a status up and every time you like, share, or comment on something. I often advise people to consider whether or not they would shout the message that they are about to broadcast on social media, over a megaphone to thousands of people. If the answer is no, I encourage them not to post. It's no different. You're still broadcasting. In fact, it is worse.

Text is often misconstrued as it lacks emphasis on tone and energy. It is quite often permanent and can be found days, weeks, months, and even years after its intended message. Be responsible for what you project. Think about everything that you do and ask yourself this question, when I type this or click this, am I becoming part of the problem or part of the solution? It's a visceral philosophy that I have in my life. You can either act as part of the problem or act as part of the solution, so which one will it be for you?

Projecting drama into the world through the internet is still projecting drama into the world, so think about making positive statements, causing positive ripple effects to your social networks and everybody else, who can see your profile, post, tweet, picture, video or comment. Everything counts, so make sure you take responsibility for all of your communication in all three types of relationships in your life.

I believe we can all achieve vast shifts in mood and happiness, through a little bit of action and a change in attitude. By taking full responsibility for every word, expression and every movement that you make as a person, you can help become a part of the solution.

#BackYourselfShare

Post a photo and tag as many of the people in your life who you know have your back! Let them know how grateful you are for them being who they are and show them that you've got their back too! Let's spread the positive vibes!

PART SIX

High Performance Mindset

This chapter will help you to perform at your best. To turn up the quality of your behaviours and start getting even better results in time management, communication, self-care, and momentum.

The majority of these tips were gathered as a result of being a dedicated student of personal development for over ten years. These habits and strategies worked amazingly well for me and now I invite you to do the same.

START YOUR DAY IN CHARGE

Start your day in charge. Those who own their day get the best results. It's as simple as that. To own your day is to stick to your own agenda and control it, free from other people distracting or diverting your valuable time, focus, and energy.

In the fast-paced world we live in, the goal is to control your time, focus, and energy at least until a chosen point in your day where you're willing to compromise. By starting your day in charge, you're able to protect your organic thoughts, feelings, ideas, and inspirations. You can set your day's intentions with clarity. The only stress present is the stress that you already know about and can approach with a clear mind.

This concept will help you to protect your time, focus, and energy so other people can't steal it from you. Starting your day in charge gives you a head start against everybody else. It gives you the edge against your competition and it helps you to become a productivity ninja. You're able to stay ahead of the tasks that come up in everyday life and also keep moving forwards with the projects you're currently working on.

The risk, if you do not start your day in charge, is that you allow other people's agendas to come into your awareness. Before you know it, the stretching of your mental bandwidth and the diverting of your attention leads to some small, subtle but seriously self-sabotaging behaviours. Your vital tasks don't get done as quickly or effectively. You're not able to put as much concentration and mental bandwidth into the things that require your attention at work or in your business, or perhaps your projects or hobbies. You suddenly close yourself in and bury yourself under a pile of new negativity, forcing you to feel differently towards people. You have mood swings, you forget what's important and you devalue the feelings of people who care about you. You may lose motivation, allow things to get in the way of your day, and before you know it, you've eaten fast food and skipped your gym session or class.

I use a simple technique in the morning to avoid these self-sabotaging circumstances. I create a 'no-phone zone' until I've got out of bed, been to the bathroom, got dressed, and sat down with my journal. In the time from my eyes opening in the morning, to sitting down with an open, blank page in my journal; I allow my mind to process my thoughts and emotions. To ponder what day it is and what important goals, actions, and tasks I need to do. I also allow myself to feel grateful for another day of life. It's mine to do whatever I want to do with it.

The journal allows me to organise, prioritise and visualise my day. It's like a form of meditation. To listen to what my mind is telling me. Pure thought. This process has been a game changer for me ever since I started doing it. Before, I would wake up, scroll my phone, get distracted, absorb the negativity from the news or social media, feel inadequate against the 'highlight reels' of other people, consume adverts and get bogged down by my emails – a list of people wanting things from me and presenting me with stress. I would STRONGLY recommend that you do this too.

It's about managing your priorities to get the essential and important tasks done without adding anything else that could potentially distract or disrupt your day. It's a great habit to have. Your time is your most valuable asset, and I'll say it again because it's one of my favourite sayings: time is the currency of life. You spend it how, when, with, and where you want to.

My intention is to help you to spend it on the tasks that are most important for your overall health, happiness, and success. Getting up early and enforcing a distraction-free morning routine is a habit that the highest performing people in the world adhere to. They do the following to enable them to have higher levels of productivity and motivation. This is what they do: they start their day with a morning routine that is bulletproof. As soon as I started to plan my ideal morning routine, my productivity levels skyrocketed.

A morning routine for a high performer looks like this:

- A good, solid six to eight hours sleep
- Get up early - so, if you're going to bed at 11:00pm or 12:00 am, you should be looking to wake up somewhere between 5:00, 6:00, 7:00 am at the latest.
- Freshen up, and get presentable to the world. No good slouching around in your PJs or your boxer shorts for an hour. Get up, get dressed, get fresh.
- The first thing that goes into your body has to be a glass of water. You need water to function at your best. Your body has just been sleeping for six to eight hours and it needs hydration. Fill yourself up with H2O, before you start thinking about the day ahead.
- Sit down and have breakfast. This isn't about nutrition right now, so whatever you consider to be a healthy breakfast, sit down and have it.
- Open up a fresh page in a notebook or a journal and write. It must be a written exercise.

At this point, I must say you have not attended to your mobile phone or your emails whatsoever. As soon as you turn on your phone to check your messages, emails, text messages, and Facebook, you become influenced by other people and therefore lose your focus and control over your own thoughts, feelings, and agenda. That is a massive danger and a massive risk, so please, I urge you, keep your phone on airplane mode at least until you're ready to tackle those external influences.

It is also no good doing your journal writing digitally through your phone or laptop or tablet. The reason for that is that we work best creatively when we're using pen to paper. This is mainly because the majority of us have been brought up learning with a pen or pencil in hand. The creativity and neuropathways in our brain are much more familiar, pure and strong when we're using pen to paper. Creativity will flow as you start to plan the tasks that are most important to you, and you start your day in charge.

What to write? For some people, it will be a full-blown task list of who they need to speak to, when they need to speak to them, what tasks need to be done, what projects are on the table, what things need to be completed at least by the end of the day. For others, it will simply be listing down six to eight things that need to be done today, no matter what.

There really is no right or wrong way. It is whatever allows you to organise, prioritise and visualise what success looks and feels like. Do it regularly and put the most important tasks and objectives down on paper. Hold yourself accountable and check in on your progress. From my experience working with lots of different people on productivity and performance, I can confidently say that those who start their day in charge go on to create success in any area of life they choose to focus on. It's part of the process that is necessary to silence the ever-present distractions we are all faced with.

The great thing is that this process can literally take five to ten minutes yet is simple and so effective. Sometimes, I will write down specific thoughts or feelings, sometimes even dreams. Other days, I simply make a list of highly important tasks or a list of names. People that I need to contact, reach out to or connect with. I may even write down a mantra or intention for the day, such as 'Today I will smile at as many people as possible'.

To get EXTRAORDINARY results, you have to be willing to do EXTRAORDINARY things. Some of the KEY HABITS I am sharing with you will take more effort and time than others, but all of them will enhance your success. Once you've owned the start of your day, organised yourself, prioritised your day, and visualised what success looks like, this is when you can invite the agendas of other people in.

I understand the urge to reach for your phone first thing in the morning. In fact, that is what so many do, but most people don't perform at an elite level, and to perform at an elite level you have to treat things differently. The reality is that the time between waking up and finishing your notes shouldn't take longer than thirty minutes (depending on how long you take to get ready).

There's nothing you need to know from anyone else in that time. In fact, even the most serious news will be dealt with in more clarity and precision AFTER you've sorted yourself out and got yourself ready for elite performance. I always advise my clients to go old school and rely on the house phone for any emergencies. Give the house phone number to anyone in your life who may need you in an emergency and tell them that you sleep with your phone off. Go on. Let go.

For you to live as your Super Self and be able to deal with anything life throws at you, you absolutely have to build new habits. The most important and valuable habit you can build tomorrow is a morning routine that allows you to take charge of your own time, focus, and energy. Protect your agenda.

- What if tomorrow you woke up a little bit earlier?
- What if tomorrow, you sat down after a glass of water, feeling fresh, clean and presentable, and you wrote down all of the important things in your day?
- What if tomorrow you kept your phone off or on airplane mode before you went to sleep?

As soon as you turn that phone on, you lose that 100% focus on your own self. You are filling your brain with the messages and demands of others. Even if it's just a small percentage, it still has an effect. Make tomorrow a more productive day by starting your day in charge until you're ready to invite the world in.

Make sure that you are the best version of yourself. It has to start with the morning. Good luck tomorrow.

 **#BackYourselfShare** Let me know how it goes. Post up a picture on Instagram looking fresh and in charge, (obviously AFTER you've done your morning routine!) and tag me @tommygentleman for proof and accountability. I would love to see how you start your day tomorrow. It will be like the first day of a new, more productive, positive and powerful life.

WHO YOU ARE IN THIS MOMENT
IS WHO YOU ARE

Your life line coincides with the universe's timeline. You share time with everyone else who is living right now. A moment is an invitation so you have the choice to show up however you'd like to. The key is to start now. Be that person, right now. This mindset application has served me so many times. Your actions in the present are YOU.

- Who are you right now?
- What is your body language saying to those around you?
- What are you wearing?
- How much self-care have you put into yourself today?

Everything that you are projecting into the world is YOU, right now in this moment and every moment in time. The time to do the things you want to do is right now. If you are the type of person who will 'do it tomorrow' then that is WHO you are. You are the guy or girl that puts it off. Would you rather be the guy or girl who gets it done? Start now, even if it's a small effort. Just start. Here's how you can do it:

- Ask yourself what kind of person you would like to be. Pick three qualities and then ask yourself what tasks you could do RIGHT NOW to demonstrate those qualities.
- Ask yourself what tasks you know you should do and what you can do RIGHT NOW to make a dent on your goals.
- Be the person who takes action.
- Be the person who leads.
- Be the person who makes it happen.
- Be the person who shows courage.

It doesn't matter if it's something new and exciting or whether it's something known and comfortable. Who you are in this moment is who you are. EVERY TIME YOU THINK OR READ IT. Show up as your Super Self.

YOU ARE ALWAYS A WORK IN PROGRESS

Often when we are working hard to achieve a change, we can be open to feelings of frustration. These feelings normally come when we become impatient or disengaged with the journey. The ultimate mindset to take is one of being 'a work in progress'.

When you know that you are doing all you can to live productively, in an honest balance, with love and in alignment with your values; you want for no more. No matter what it is you are working towards, you will always restore your belief and your patience when you know you are a work in progress. Nobody is perfect and we are on an ever-evolving journey.

As long as you know you are making moves, you can go easier on yourself and trust the process. When you are a work in progress, your success becomes inevitable. You could look at your body, your bank account, your ring finger, or any situation and apply the belief that 'I am a work in progress' to instantly reduce the frustration.

Nothing of stature is achieved in an instant. It's the compound effect of daily choices and actions over a consistent and considerably long period of time. That is the process, and you are always learning. You'll get there eventually. It's happening and you are doing it. All that stands in your way is time. **So, keep putting one foot in front of the other and you'll inevitably get there. Enjoy the journey.**

BE RELENTLESS

An essential ingredient for success is hard work. Most people know this already and it is something that is widely expressed on social media, on podcasts, and in books. What people don't tend to share is that in order to be successful, one must be relentless. Working hard isn't good enough. Many people work hard. Some work harder than others while some people work smarter than others, but those who are relentless in the pursuit of their goals are the ones who will ultimately win long-term.

Being relentless means that you are willing to go the extra distance. To ask the crunchy questions, muck in yourself when you need to, get up early, and stay up late until it's done. One can only truly find their relentless streak when they are under pressure. That's what separates the winners from the talkers.

You can have all the best interests, manners, and ambitions when things are good, but when you are under pressure it changes the harmony of the situation and in those pressure moments you must be relentless if you are to be one of the few who breaks through and get extraordinary results.

113

How your values show up under pressure is the real test of who you are. You have probably heard of the phrase 'You have to be hungry for success.' This saying derives from a time when people would literally go hungry unless they figured out how to get food. They would have to do whatever it took to get fed. Although this may not be the actual scenario you find yourself in, you must take the same approach. Realise what is at stake, pair that with your strongest reason why and then work relentlessly to make it happen. Make your health and happiness a part of your survival standards.

Raise the bar beyond simply existing and be relentless in your pursuit of success for the sake of you and your family.

BELONG TO THE TRIBE OF TRUTH

The truth always comes out in the end and honesty is the best policy. Two very well-known cliché statements, but they are both absolutely bang on correct. When your own energy is pure, you integrate seamlessly with the powers that surround you.

Lying is tiring, you have to constantly retrace your actions and be so sensitive and aware of being exposed. Living in the tribe of truth is to be 100% accountable for your own actions. More opportunities come your way and you have less reason to look over your shoulder. To speak from the heart and to always back yourself in any given situation. To not treat people like lesser beings but to embrace the equality we each share in the form of time and space itself. We are all connected and our energy blends together to balance the forces of the universe. I feel so strongly about this and do my best to live a heightened, released, and pure life.

Bring the tribe of truth into your life. Your work, relationships, sport, goals, the way you dress, the way you speak, the words you use, the way you walk into a room, the promises you make and, of course, when you are being challenged and life is testing your patience.

The truth is linear. It has no frayed edges or weak points. It's strong and it's an extension of who you are. The truth will always serve you in the long run.

PART SEVEN

Miracles: The Extra Ingredient

WHAT IS A MIRACLE?

We have all been presented with miracles in our lives, but only some choose to notice. It has taken me a few years to finally accept miracles can happen and they are very much real. The three examples I will share with you are each a personal story of mystery and power.

Sometimes, we don't need to find an explanation. That beautiful grey area between scientific fact and religious belief. Both science and religion were both born from the same question. Why are we here? Humanity has evolved with this very question on our lips throughout our entire conscious existence. I am not a religious person, but I am spiritual. I believe in a higher power, a divine energy that exists in both science and faith. I believe it to be a factor of space, time, and energy.

The human senses are limited to five and within these amazing senses, we can only process a small amount of information. There are frequencies that we cannot sense and since we cannot sense them, how do we know they exist?'

I stopped trying to prove the black and white of things a few years ago when I had my first experience of a 'miracle' and those since then which helped me to succeed against the weight of life and the pull of depression. To not include them would be to hold back from you and I can't hold back. All that I ask is that you approach with an open mind.

FINDING FAITH - FEATHERS & FOOTBALLS

I was fortunate enough to know all four of my grandparents. My dad's parents grew up in the East End of London, lived through World War Two, and gave us grandchildren so much love. Dad's mum is still alive and a beautiful human being. Her husband (my grandad) passed away two years prior to me writing this book.

My grandad on my mum's side was a WO2 officer in the British Army. He was six foot four and had a powerful presence but a compassionate heart. My mum's mum passed away when I was fifteen. She was an amazing Japanese woman with a caring heart. She lived through the Hiroshima bombing and always had a soft smile on her face.

All four of them had seen far more pain and struggle than me by the time they were my age. I often think back and wonder how the hell they managed to give us so much love having been through so much heartbreak. Losing loved ones to random bombings, sharing bedrooms with up to six other siblings, having to bury way too many friends and family members and all before they had a chance to live a full life. I always respect my elders and I never take for granted what they would have had to have been through to help provide me and my generation with the opportunities we have in our lives.

When my nan died, it was my first experience of grief and loss. In times of struggle in my early adult life, I would go and visit her grave to seek guidance. I had learned from a friend of my mum's that a white feather could be a sign from heaven. A symbol that those who could no longer be with us in physical form were still watching over us, sending us a reminder of their love and helping to show us the right direction.

I can remember one day in my late teens, I was struggling to find clarity and purpose in my life. I felt sad and lonely, and so I went to seek comfort at my nan's grave. Living the majority of her life as a Buddhist meant it was placed in a special line dedicated to those who weren't of Christian belief.

I sat there, feeling low and upset and I asked for a sign, "If you can hear me, show me a sign."

I felt so stupid saying those words out loud but the way I saw it, that I had nothing to lose. After waiting for a few minutes and nothing happening, I had a final look around in desperation and then decided that was that. I stood up and walked away. I felt a cold void of disbelief coupled with the mild embarrassment that I would even consider asking for a sign. How crazy does that sound?

As I went to open the door of my car, I turned around and looked back at the grave. I couldn't quite believe my eyes. There was a distinct print on the grass area where I had been sat, and on top of the impression was a beautiful white feather. I picked it up, smiled, and got into my car. Could it be coincidence? Yes, it could. Could it be a sign? Yes, it could. Are the two connected? Yes, possibly. It was enough to give me some hope. I went home and put the feather on my bedroom wall. My first miracle. From that moment on I had an open mind.

Five years later I found myself in the same cemetery, sat on that same patch of grass. The only difference, this time there were two tombstones. Jamie's memorial was placed next to my nan's. It allowed us to go and pay our respects to them both every time we visited the cemetery. Knowing they were close gave us some comfort.

I picked up the ball, put the feathers in my pocket, and took them home. To this day, both the ball and the feathers are together at my parents' house in Jamie's old bedroom. This moment changed my life. I accepted, truly accepted there must be other forces at play around us that we cannot see, hear, touch, taste, or smell. Our senses are limited to a small percentage of brain usage. For centuries, science and religion have been trying to find answers and evidence. I now had mine.

A TEXT MESSAGE FROM HEAVEN

Dealing with death never disappears. It changes over time but it never fully heals. Seven years on aged twenty-seven, I was having a tough time and missing my brother.

The hardest part is thinking about what could have been. I had just got married and I wished so much for him to have been there with us in person. I had most certainly matured and evolved, but despite having love in my life through my family, my wife, and my work, I would still struggle from time to time.

I went for a drive one morning in between clients to clear my head. I had just got myself a new car, my first brand new one, a Volkswagen Tiguan. I am not a petrol head whatsoever and if I am honest, the main reason I chose a Tiguan was that the first three letters are the same as my initials (TIG).

My last client told me it was possible to connect my phone so my text messages would show up on the dash screen. Before I set off for my drive, I configured my phone and syncronised my device with the car. Ten minutes into the drive I received a text message. Curiously, I pressed the message button on the dash screen and what I saw almost made me crash my car! The name of the sender: JAMEE.

When Jamie got his first mobile phone, I saved his number as 'Jamee'. We both found it amusing at the time and partly through sensitivity, I had kept his number saved on my phone even seven years later. I pulled over at the side of the road. Confused and emotional, I clicked to open the message. I am not sure what I expected to see. Surely it was a technical glitch and not a message from Jamie himself. I mean, anything is possible, right?

I read the message. It was from Kelly. "That's strange," I thought. Straight away I needed to find out what was going on. I rang Kelly immediately and told her what had happened. I asked her to text me again. The same thing happened, 'Message from Jamee.'

"It must be a problem with the contact synchronization?" I said to Kelly.

Just then, another message came through. It was from my cousin Niko. I opened it and sure enough, it was really from Niko.

"There can't be a contact sync issue, otherwise Niko's message would have read someone else's name?"

In the end, I submitted to yet again another miracle. Another influencing of communication through energies that cannot be defined or proven. This exceptional day reminded me to stay on track and to keep the faith in miracles. Some things just don't need an explanation from anyone other than yourself.

SPIRITUAL GUIDANCE

I have always felt a strong pull towards my Japanese heritage.

I have a very large Japanese dragon tattooed on my right thigh. The tattoo was designed and applied by a Japanese artist in London and took fifteen hours in total over four separate trips to the studio in Shoreditch. The dragon was to remind me of my power and heritage and to keep the message that not everything needs to be 'real' for it to exist. Especially a miracle. It was important for me to have this permanent symbol applied by a Japanese artist. It just felt right. I was feeling pulled into my Japanese heritage. It felt strange, like a journey of self-discovery that had woken up inside of me. I felt this tattoo would be something highly significant and important for me to remember and live by every single day.

I knew that I wanted to represent the same special meaning of this tattoo within this book. I wanted it to be a part of the book's philosophy and so I had the same artist design the Dragon crest that you see on the cover and on all of the #BackYourselfShare pages! (That's what it means in case you were wondering!)

Around the same time as I got this tattoo, I had started my second martial art, Japanese Ju Jitsu. I wanted to move like my ancestors. It felt like I was speaking a familiar language and I soon made my way through the ranks. At the start and finish of every lesson, we would do some focus breathing exercises to channel our energy and clear our mind.

One night, after a heavy, heated, and testing lesson, I lined up on my knees to partake in the routine breathing exercise. My heart was pounding and my body was lit from a physical and empowering session As I closed my eyes and took a deep breath in through my nose, a figure presented himself in my mind's eye.

I was vibrating at such a level in my life that under the circumstances of my ancestors I had opened up an awareness to what I could only describe as a guardian angel. The figure stood in a dark street with a black cloak on and a large circular samurai's hat covering his face. He had a purple force field around him and stood still and focused. He had a sense of power and was ready for battle, yet calm in his stance.

It felt like he was right in front of me. As if he was revealing himself to my awareness and paying respect towards me for being on my journey in life. The vision lasted for a few seconds and then disappeared.

What was that...I felt an incredible rush of excitement and purpose and an overwhelming message of 'You are in the right place' came over me. This inner power had revealed itself and I still didn't understand what the hell it was, but it felt *right*.

Despite trying many times through meditation and concentrated thought, I really couldn't recall the figure in my mind after the day he first showed up. However, the figure remained a memory and an inspired idea until a warm February day in San Diego. I had agreed to go to on a business trip with two mentors of mine and another of their students. The trip had come a week after my first Super Self Summit. Life was at an all-time high and I had established myself as a Speaker and Event host.

I had been chasing this dream for almost eight years and had my fair share of knockbacks. After investing a lot of time, energy, and money in the journey, I had finally BECOME that person with money in the bank, love in my heart, and a level of peace in my mind that I had not had before.

The four of us were sat in an outdoor bar on Coronado island that overlooked the beach. It was a beautiful day and the sun was just starting to set into the sea. I closed my eyes and felt the warmth of the sun on my face.

I started to tap my feet to the trance-like sounds of ambient music and began to feel my vibration increase. Then it happened. In my mind's eye, I saw him again. My Samurai warrior presenting himself after years of being dormant. This time, he lifted his hat and showed me his eyes. They were sharp, yet dark. Almost as if they had an infinite space inside of them. *What did this mean? Why now? Is it even real or just my imagination?*

I had to go with my gut instinct and take note. They pierced my awareness. "I have to go inside," I said to the others as I opened my eyes and stood up. I had felt a compelling need to stand up and walk into the small boutique shopping centre. I followed my instincts, not knowing why or what I was looking for. As I walked into the first shop, I felt like I was being led to something important.

It was a men's clothing store that specialised in designer suits and shirts. I walked around, looking for a significant sign. Something that would stick out as obvious relevance to me and act as a reason for my spontaneous actions. A part of me felt stupid at the fact that I was walking around a shop being led by a Samurai warrior spiritual guide looking for a sign! But I continued anyway.

I had walked around the entire shop but I had seen nothing remotely close to a sign. Yet the whole time I felt deep down I would see something. I felt he was showing me he has my back and that I had taken my life to a level that deserved more knowledge as to who and what he is. I made a point of speaking to the handful of people in the shop, but none of them lit up to my presence.

It's not the people that hold the message...
So what is it?
Maybe there isn't one...

I was about to leave the shop, when I noticed a small walkway up into a tiny section of the shop that I hadn't yet explored. As you can imagine, I was intrigued. I smiled and just KNEW that what I had been looking for would be up there. As I walked up the ramp, I saw something incredible.

Hanging on the wall right in front of me like a monument above an altar was a shirt that had a stunning Samurai warrior stitched on the back. I felt like shouting YES! But instead, I resisted, closed my eyes and softly said, "thank you." I believe. I took a photo of the shirt and walked back to my friends in complete contentment.

Ever since that moment, I have been on a conscious journey of spiritual discovery and I have been learning more and more about the amazing theories of energy, the soul, afterlife, and the universe. I know part of my path will be to share more of my discoveries with you in the future and to help you find that little bit extra power and purpose in your life.

When you believe it is even POSSIBLE there are external forces at play that we cannot detect with our very limited human senses, a whole universe of hope, faith and love opens up. For some this is religion, for others it is something else. It doesn't matter 'what it is' only that it exists and you invite the miracles.

The universe speaks to us all. Some of us ignore its message, others are learning to listen, and then there are those who embrace it and dance with it.

PART EIGHT

Legacy

The final chapter of Back Yourself.

In this chapter, I invite you to begin thinking about your LEGACY. What does it all mean to you and what will you be remembered for?

I believe that we all die twice. Once when you stop breathing and life leaves your body, and then again when you are mentioned or thought about for the last time in human history.

WHAT IS LEGACY?

Legacy to me is the result of our actions in life that will exist beyond our death. Each of us is living our legacy. What we do with our time will determine how much of an impact we will have on the world once we have gone.

Many human beings just like you and I have been immortalised within their legacy by doing extraordinary things that have changed the course of the world or highly influenced popular culture. A legacy can be achieved by consciously 'trying' to achieve big goals. It can also be achieved by just doing your thing. The sweet spot is to marry the two.

I witnessed LEGACY at Jamie's funeral. This boy had made such an impression on people that he filled the biggest church in town with over seven hundred people in attendance at his funeral. He may not have even known what legacy was. His love and essence has allowed his name to live on in our hearts and in the charity we set up after he died. We have raised over £200,000 to help increase youth participation in sport in our local area and continue to spread his legacy year on year. Children get to try different sports because of HIM. They can find their passion and possibly even go on to spread their own legacy within that activity. Thanks to Jamie's own legacy.

Legacy will occur for us all. What we do in our life will determine what we are remembered for, how long we are remembered and by how many people. It's your actions today that will shape your legacy tomorrow.

ENJOY YOURSELF & HAVE FUN

I set up my first business in 2009. A small personal training studio 200 feet behind my parents' house. Infin8pulse was like nothing that had ever been seen before, it was a studio with gym equipment, a treatment room, an office, toilet, and a kitchen.

I teamed up with two good friends who shared my vision, Andy Hillier, who I worked with previously before I moved to NZ and Terry Anderson who I knew from school. For two years, we did our thing. Having a personal trainer was almost unheard of back then. Especially in Andover. We created a culture and built our respective client bases.

We ran early morning bootcamps and group programs and I believe we were far ahead of our time. Things were good but I wanted more. Although I had no idea how I would do it or where I would even start, I started plans to open a gym. A gym would be a completely different experience.

For a start, the sheer size required would constitute a huge increase in rent and rates. There would be substantial running costs, car parking requirements, refurbishment costs, and staffing. I often think that if I knew what I know now back then, I may have reconsidered! But nothing was going to stop me. I had it set in my mind and I was determined to make it happen. I found a suitable unit and had begun constructing a business plan. I wanted to create a gym where everybody felt comfortable and confident in doing their thing.

No intimidation, no judgment, just inspired health and fitness. I wanted to capture the essence of life and celebrate how unique we all are yet we all require a healthy protocol in order to live longer and healthier. Everyone has their own motivation. Their own purpose. Their own REASON.

The planning permission for Reasons Fitness took six months. We needed change of use on the building to comply with town council regulations. I did the application process myself. It took a lot out of me and after many late-night admin sessions and council meetings, we finally heard the great news. It had been accepted.

All that had to be done now was to confirm the financial support required to see the project through. With legal costs, deposits and refurbishment costs, plus two months' worth of cash flow to help support the initial phase, I needed to find some more money. So far, I had managed to save forty percent of what I needed with the collaborative efforts of my parents and myself. But I was short.

I went to speak to one of my mentors in life and in business, Grandad Rowe aka 'Big John'. My mum's dad had a commanding presence and compassionate heart. He had served maximum time in the army and had completed various tours to Borneo, Hong Kong, and fought in the Korean War.

Upon leaving the army, he unleashed his entrepreneurial side and had made multiple investments as well as starting his own business providing rubber stamp solutions locally. He taught me so much about money. His lessons in work ethic were distinctly memorable. I would be sent to his house on Saturdays to carry out some simple tasks in exchange for some pocket money. Grandad got it right. He worked me hard, but he paid well.

He taught me that work isn't slavery. You don't have to bust your balls to be entitled to a few pennies. When you bust your balls, you get paid equal to your effort. However, if the work wasn't up to standard, you got NOTHING and you had to keep working.

I can remember one day he had me weed his garden and sweep up the leaves. I had been working for two hours and I was tired. I must have been around nine years old at the time. Some of the leaves were stuck to the ground by last night's rain, and the weeds were so rigid they were hurting my fingers. I told him I had finished and he came out to check.

He shook his head and said to me, "You are not finished at all. There are still leaves on the ground and there are still weeds between the cracks of the patio. Next time you come and get me, these must be pulled out and the rest of the leaves swept away."

I reluctantly carried on for another hour or so before going back to get him. He came out, nodded, and said, "That's better well done. Hold out your hand, here's £10. Save it."

It makes me smile now thinking about it. I was blessed to have had such positive influence around me as a child. Both sets of grandparents and my parents. Six strong positive people giving me input on my journey and helping to nurture the person I would become.

The week I had arranged to sit down and talk business with my grandad, he was taken ill and moved to a hospital ward. My Mum had told me that they suspected bowel cancer. We went to visit him in Winchester hospital. It was the first time I had been to this hospital since Jamie passed away within the same walls.

Grandad was lying in a hospital bed, alert and in good spirits. Nobody really knew what was happening. My uncle and my mum were also in the room. There was a knock at the door and in walked the doctor with news.

My grandad sat up and began to listen to the doctor as he started talking medical jargon and hypothesising over what it would mean if x happened or y happened. Big John, a military veteran hero who for his whole life had oozed courage and led people into dangerous and hostile environments whilst installing and maintaining focus and faith, was now facing his biggest mission report to date.

The information was going in, but it wasn't what he wanted to hear. The doctor finished his final sentence and my grandad looked him square in the eyes and with a stern and controlled tone he asked, "Doctor, just tell me how long I have?"

The doctor had already explained that he, "Wouldn't like to comment" but could not resist Big John's authority and courageous charm.

"Between four and six weeks," he said solemnly as he nodded his head and maintained eye contact.

My grandad didn't even flinch. He smiled, and then simply held out his big hand to which the doctor reciprocated, they shook hands and the doctor left the room.

Even having been served his terms, this war hero wanted to fight until the very end. He was moved to a hospice on the same road as his house. A house he would never see again. I visited him every day in the hospice.

He was in good spirits, handling his business, moving his money ready to set his three children and five grandchildren up for the future. He was managing his financial legacy from his deathbed. He insisted on knowing all of my business plans. He wanted to help me as much as he could whilst he was able. One morning, I went to visit him to show him the new logo I had had designed that incorporated our Japanese family crest. He loved it and even wanted me to have a T-shirt made for him with the new logo on.

We talked business and he wrote me a cheque. I was incredibly grateful for his generosity. It made it so that I didn't need to borrow as much money from the bank. It brought me closer to my target. The next time I went to visit, would be the last time. We had received the phone call to say 'come now'.

This was the third time I had had such a call. I saw my nan in her last hours at fifteen years old. I had rushed to hospital but not seen my brother Jamie when I was only twenty years old. In that moment I was heading to see my grandad for the last time at twenty-three years old.

He was laying in his hospice bed, struggling to breathe. My mum, uncle and cousins were there and Jeni had been informed in New Zealand. I sat right next to him.

A rush of thoughts came into my mind and reminded me of our incredible mortality. This man who I had looked up to my whole life, a hero, a beacon of courage and love was dying in front of my eyes. I felt sad and I was scared, but at the same time, I also felt a soft appreciation for life and death.

Having had the fortunate opportunity and gut feeling to tell Jamie that I was proud of him in our last moments together, I knew I needed to do the same now. I was scared. I held my grandad's hand as he struggled to breathe. He had his eyes closed and wasn't responding. 'Say it. What are you waiting for?' rang on repeat in my head. 'You will regret this forever this is the last time you will ever get to speak to him!' Yet still, I wouldn't open my mouth.

I knew that I was running out of time and holding onto my words. This was it. For what? Fear? I held his hand and leant over to speak into his ear.

"Grandad, I love you."

I have only been to see Jamie's memorial a handful of times. I normally reserve the trip for times when I feel the most amount of sadness or hurt. Or when I am seeking guidance and contemplation. This one particular time I had been sat looking for answers for over thirty minutes. I had recently started dating Kelly and I was struggling with opening up. Kelly didn't know Jamie.

Jamie was such a big part of my life and his death dominated my thinking for at least three years. Kelly was a big part of my life too. An exciting breath of fresh air that I was struggling to embrace due to my own fear of getting hurt. I sat at the grave, thinking and searching for guidance. Again I asked for a sign, "I know this is a lot to ask, and I do believe, but if you can hear me, please give me another sign."

This time it felt even more bizarre. I should have just taken the first miracle as evidence and got on with things. But no, I asked the question. I had no expectation, but deep down I craved hope.

Nothing happened. I waited. Still nothing. So, I got up and left. Of course, as I went to get in my car, I checked behind me. Just in case. Nothing. I smiled and thought to myself, "well, that was pushing my luck I suppose." I got into my car and I drove around a small roundabout towards the exit. As I turned the corner, I noticed something out of the corner of my eye. On a wide stretch of green grass, there lay a round white object. It was a football.

"That's strange." I stopped the car, got out, and walked up to the ball. What happened next, I can only put down to a divine miracle of hope and faith. Gently resting on the top of the football were two beautiful white feathers gracefully intertwined with each other. Needless to say, I was struck. I dropped to my knees and started crying. Then I started laughing!

He hadn't been responsive for a while but he opened his eyes. He raised his other arm and placed his hand on top of mine. He smiled, looked me in the eyes with that same leader-like love and authority and somehow managed to bring up the strength to mutter the words, "I know. Just enjoy yourself. Have fun."

The last message of a man who had taught me so much. I admire the way my grandad captured his legacy. He lived with intention and power. He looked after us and he created a financial plan to help his loved ones benefit from his life's work.

He was surrounded by love in his last moments and although there would have inevitably been some darkness from his military days, I like to imagine that his final thoughts would have been of gratitude and appreciation for his life, his journey, and all of the adventures he had experienced. He taught me that EVERYTHING COUNTS.

I continued with my plans to open the gym a few months later. The t-shirt I had made for him rode with him in the back of the hearse. It hung for all to see at his funeral. The torch had been passed and the chief had moved on.

Big John left inheritance money for us all. My Mum agreed to place some of hers, and I put up all of mine, and the finance for the gym was complete. Looking back, I know that my grandad could have written me a cheque for the full amount, but knew that he was going to die and leave the money anyway. Perhaps he wanted to test my gratitude and give me one final lesson.

The very first thing I did when we opened Reasons Fitness was have his t-shirt framed and hung on the wall as a reminder. He helped me bring it all into existence. I can only hope to emulate his impact in life and in death. A powerful example of legacy.

WHAT'S NEXT?

I am writing this chapter on September 21st, 2018.

This morning, Kelly and I visited the ultrasound department in our local hospital, two rooms down from where Lincoln was born. We are thirteen weeks pregnant. Seeing the baby on the screen was a thing of beauty.

It felt a lot more enjoyable than last time, probably because we had an idea of the process. In six months time, I'll have another baby. It'll most likely be just after this book gets launched. Who knows what is in store for us. To the world, another human being. Another name, another statistic and another resource. To us, LEGACY.

What can one man or woman achieve in their life? Anything. All of our heroes are human beings just like us and our future children. I'm excited for our little family to grow and it has strengthened my purpose. I'm happy for Kelly and our parents too. More reason to be happy. As well as family, this book, and my clients, I will be running more personal development events and continuing to express myself in various ways.

So what about you? At this stage, I would like to say at the end what I said to you at the beginning, "I want you to know that it doesn't matter where you are at right now and that the distance between your current challenge and the possible victory is not to be looked at as a frustration but as an exciting opportunity."

It probably won't ever be easy but it can be a lot easier. There will always be a level of randomness to life and it is very possible that you will have a fair share of challenges. But that is no reason to hold back. When the road is clear, you go. Fast and enjoy the ride.

When there's a roadblock, you figure out how to get around it, over it, or through it. Giving up is not an option.

For as long as your heart is beating, you have the opportunity of life and the choice of your own attitude. Your life will continue to be a learning process and you can help make it easier by continuing to invest in yourself. Invest time, energy, focus, and money in your own journey. Read, watch, study, listen and go to live events. Every time you learn something, you invest in YOURSELF.

Progress is not something we are entitled to. We get rewarded for the effort we put in. Our effort shapes our success and by investing in yourself, you will continue to craft your results. An investment in yourself can never be taken away. Time itself protects your investment, and action is what brings it into reality.

You could put this book down, store the inspiration you have gained, and do nothing with it;

Or,

You could start getting to work one small action at a time. It starts with an ATTITUDE shift. You have the power, the ability, and the potential to BACK YOURSELF. To be the one who takes full responsibility and becomes the true creator of happiness. To live in line with your values and enjoy yourself, so much so that what you create leaves a legacy which outlives your mortal clock. There are no more excuses. Nothing or nobody to blame. No more duff-hands or tones of 'poor me'. It's all you.

You are an amazing and unique creation of beauty. The opportunity is just too good to miss. There will never be anybody like you in the history of the world. Never has been and never will be, and THAT is why you should always BACK YOURSELF.

GO!

This is where I call you out.

You've read my book and for that, I am truly grateful. Too many people are experts in 'shelf-development' and don't follow through with the actual self-development, so well done.

Now, I want to challenge you for one last time on this particular phase of our journey together.

You are going to write a statement of intent for yourself. A message that will hold you accountable for the next 365 days. Here's how to do it:

Write today's date on a blank piece of paper and then just let your pen flow. Put today's date at the top and then write the following line to get you started...

"This time next year I will ..."

Then write down something about your health, relationships, career/business, mindset, energy, confidence, situations, finances, and levels of happiness. When you are finished, seal it in an envelope and address it to yourself, to open exactly one year from today.

This is a personal and private statement, however, I WOULD LOVE to see a photo of you holding your envelope or simply holding your copy of the book.

Either send it to me privately at tommy@backyourselfbook.com

Or post it up online with the hashtag **#BackYourselfShare** so that myself and the Back Yourself community can get behind you!

It'll also be a great accountability move to support your goals. I look forward to seeing what you share!

I would love to hear from you regarding anything else that I can possibly help you with. I wrote this book with your best interests in my mind and my heart. So, please do let me know how this book has helped you along your journey. Maybe one day I will get to meet you at one of my events.

All of my news and updates will feature on my website. Visit www.tommygentleman.com for all my events, books, courses and programs.

Remember, there are supporting videos and some exclusive additional coaching content over at www.backyourselfbook. com/bonus

THANK YOU

The writing of this book began back in 2010.

I started by scribbling down some of my thoughts and feelings. I knew that I wanted to help people and inspire people with the lessons and discoveries that I had made as a result of going through a life changing tragedy.

The relationship between self expression and providing helpful value is one that any Author fights with.

The problem that I always came up against was the WHY.

To share something so personal with the world would require a strong reason and a genuine motive.

The time didn't seem right back in 2010.

It was too soon and I was too young.

I tried again in 2015.

But this time, I was motivated too greatly by the commercial gain and social exposure that the words never really seemed to flow together.

Then, in 2018, I finally wrote the book.

Many factors have come together for this to be the PERFECT time for me to do this. Turning 30, having a child, launching a personal development company, having the time and even growing my hair!

All roads have come together to shape my IDENTITY.

The person that I am today is ready to handle the responsibility and shares his message in a way that is authentic and purposeful.

To myself I say...

You did it!

Hold everything that has ever happened close in your heart, as these moments, good or bad have shaped you and form your legacy.

But let today be the closing of a deep chapter that you would never have chosen, but upon being dealt, you chose to live.

To you I say...

Thank you for being here.

Thank you for being you.

Your energy is what drives me. The sparkle of life in your eye is what lights me up. Your heart, your mind and your unique face is what makes this world so amazing.

We are all connected and we are all a part of something truly incredible.

Keep learning.
Keep smiling.
Keep doing you.

Yours in health & happiness,
Tommy Gentleman

16581392R00087

Printed in Great Britain
by Amazon